Beautiful
Deception

By
Yasmeen Suri

Thank you Lord for giving me the patience
and endurance to write this book.

May it accomplish Your will in the lives
of men and women in Jesus name…amen.

"But as for you, teach what accords with sound doctrine."

Titus 2:1, ESV

Contents

—⁓⁕⁓—

Introduction

-–◦৩⟩✝⟨৫৩–-

Beauty can be a door to deception, a doorway where the enemy can gain access. This present portal remains undetected by many in the world and the church. Deception comes in many forms and the deadliest is the beauty that is "disguised" either physically or spiritually. Poets rave about beauty. Brave men have started wars over beauty. Women in the world over strive for it. Scholars devote their lives to deconstructing our impulse to obtain it. Ordinary mortals erect temples to beauty. In just about every way imaginable the world honors physical beauty, and the church honors spiritual beauty. Even beauty, however, can become a deadly and deceptive ideal if it leads us outside the authority of the truth of the scriptures in the Holy Bible.

Psychological research reveals that an indiscriminate comparison of feminine beauty affects men's feelings about their current partner. Viewing pictures of attractive women weakens their commitment to their mates. Men rate themselves as being less attracted and even less in love with their partner after looking at *Playboy* centerfolds than they did before seeing the pictures of beautiful women. Sociologists and social psychologists have long known that there is a widespread perception that physically attractive people are more intelligent, more competent, and possess other more desirable characteristics. A large number of experiments over the years have shown that, when asked to rate the intelligence or competence of unknown subjects, people tend to rate attractive subjects as more intelligent and competent than those who are less attractive.

Consider what might happen to a person if he or she were extremely beautiful. Consider further what might happen if he or she were not only beautiful but also highly intelligent. Then consider what might happen if this person attained a high position in the world of business or politics. It does not take much imagination to see that he or she might likely become intensely proud of his or her beauty and intelligence. He or she might likely feel superior to others and likely to desire greater power, wealth, and prestige, becoming increasingly self-centered and self-seeking as his or her greed and pride grew. This experience has happened over and over again to people who were not even the most beautiful or the most intelligent.

In the end times the Bible warns us of a great deception that will come to the inhabitants of the earth. People will be deceived because they do not have a love for the truth found in God's Word. Instead their desire to run their lives according to their own ways will be the foundation of deception. Pride is the core of all rebellion. *"Pride goes before destruction, a haughty spirit before a fall.* (Proverbs 16:18, NIV) This is what happened to Satan.

For an example, just watch the commercials during the Super Bowl. During the NFL event, there comes on television, the super-original fantasy of having a bunch of nearly-nude fembots (female robots) mindlessly standing at attention in the background in case they are needed to fulfill the sexual fantasies of average-Joe-millionaires.

Beauty can be deceptive in many forms and it can be used for either good or evil. The word "evil" refers specifically to the policy of Satan as the ruler of this world. Evil has been the modus operandi of Satan from the time of his fall, throughout the angelic revolution, and down to the point when he became the ruler of this world; a dark under-lord wielding power over the created order itself (2 Corinthians 4:4). From the beginning beauty was found in the Garden of Eden. God's creation was perfect, immortal and without corruption—until the disobedience of Adam and Eve imparted imperfection, mortality and corruption into the created order itself (Romans 5:12). The agent of this violation of God's order was Satan himself whose original power, majesty and beauty was revealed in Ezekiel 28:11-13, *"Moreover the word of the LORD came unto me, saying, Son of man, take up a lamentation upon the king of Tyrus, and say unto him, Thus saith the LORD God; Thou sealest up the sum, full of wisdom, and perfect in beauty. Thou hast been in Eden the garden of God. . . ."* (KJV)

You see, Satan himself was responsible for his transformation into the being we now call the devil by the development of his pride, greed, arrogance, and self-seeking ambition. These caused him to plunge into an immoral and carnal state while retaining his essential glory and beauty. Verse 15 of Ezekiel 28 says, "till iniquity was found in thee", to which this refers. God created a perfect, holy angel named Lucifer (Isaiah 14:12), and that angel became the being we now call the devil.

The question is sometimes asked, "Why did God create this angel who would become the devil?" When God created beings with a free will, He knew that sooner or later, one of them would begin to experience pride and selfish ambition just as Satan did. The choice to do evil, in this case, is to yield to pride and self. It is still always a choice. Satan was responsible for his own transformation, choosing his course and deliberately rebelling against the very glory of God Himself, with full knowledge of what he was doing. Isaiah 14:12-15 really shows how Lucifer became Satan:

> *"How art thou fallen from heaven, O Lucifer, son of the morning! How art thou cut down to the ground, which didst weaken the nations! For thou hast said in thine heart, I will ascend into heaven, I will exalt my throne above the stars of God: I will sit also upon the mount of the congregation, in the sides of the north: I will ascend above the heights of the clouds; I will be like the most High. Yet thou shalt be brought down to hell, to the sides of the pit. (KJV)*

Note how many times the Word of the Lord reveals that Satan willfully chose to rebel! The most beautiful of creatures, and closest to the throne of God, and what does he do? He chooses! God gave him a "free will" to choose.

Satan is directly opposed to anything involving the Lord Jesus Christ. Satan is devoted to distorting or obscuring any truth related to Christ.

> *"And even if our gospel is veiled, it is veiled to those who are perishing, in whose case the god of this world has blinded the minds of the unbelieving, that they might not see the light of the gospel of the glory of Christ, who is the image of God." (2 Corinthians 4:3-4, NASB)*

Through evil, Satan brings about two major consequences on earth: sin and human good (the motivation of evil), both of which are based on errors in thinking. The sin of self-righteousness combined with human good or sincerity produces a saturation of evil in a nation.

One of the main reasons for learning about evil from the Bible is to learn that man cannot solve his problems by human solutions. Any effective solution to a human problem is a divine solution. And there is an answer in the Bible for every human need or problem. What we call "beauty", is a powerful influence which is neither good, nor evil, but readily exploited by the world, the flesh, and the devil himself to magnify deception on so many levels. Read Romans 7:7-13 on how sin itself uses the holy to compel us to plunge into disobedience, just as deception uses the beautiful to move us to do things we might never otherwise consider doing. The beautiful voices of our famous rock stars and contemporary singers promote lust and rebellion as much as Barbie dolls are an example to encourage lust for little girls. The dolls are hardly dressed and bare bodies are exposed to encourage nudity and immodesty.

"Favour is deceitful, and beauty is vain: but a woman that feareth the LORD, she shall be praised." (Proverbs 31:30 , NASB)

Ignorance comes with a high price. It is written in the Bible, *But the Lord said to Samuel, "Do not look on his appearance or on the height of his stature, because I have rejected him. For the Lord sees not as man sees: man looks on the outward appearance, but the Lord looks on the heart."* (1 Samuel 16:7, ESV). This means that neither beauty, nor unattractiveness, can necessarily be equated with goodness or righteousness. The Lord looks on the heart of a man. Not his appearance.

We do also understand that if someone, or something, looks "evil" or even "unholy", it is common sense to judge that it most likely is. God may also give us the gift of "discerning of spirits" which is one of the gifts of the Holy Spirit as found in 1 Corinthians 12:10. This is spiritual gift given supernaturally by God to discern between the operations of God's Spirit, an evil spirit, or some other impulse.

We are naturally drawn to beauty physically, emotionally and spiritually. This book will take you through a series of natural and spiritual examples and examine the deceptive lure in which when beauty is disguised in many facets, it can either destroy or bless an individual's life. After reading this book, one will be able to grow and learn to discern the difference according to God's Word.

Chapter 1

In Worship...

—⚜—

While I was sleeping during the night hours, I had an interesting dream. In my dream I was taken into outer space while the entire earth was below me. I also saw the heavens far into the midst of the galaxy. I knew Lord was with me even though I could not see Him. As I was looking, the earth became a living, breathing round form. I was watching it breathing in and out almost like a lung. While I was watching, I was so astonished and I asked without speaking, "Lord, what am I seeing?" He said, "You are seeing the earth worshipping." I thought to myself, "worshipping?" I looked closer and I heard and saw the sounds of worship. Then I realized most of the worship was not going to the Lord but to the devil. As I looked closer, I said, "Lord...where are you servants?" He said, "They are washed with white robes and the mark of the red blood stained cross is upon them." I looked closer into the earth and I was searching for the worshippers of the Most High God and I was shocked that they were so far and few. They were so difficult to find. Then immediately I awoke out of the dream.

"And you he made alive, when you were dead through the trespasses and sins in which you once walked, following the course of this world, following the prince of the power of the air, the spirit that is now at work in the sons of disobedience. Among these we all once lived in the passions of our flesh, following the desires of body and mind, and so we were by nature children of wrath, like the rest of mankind." (Ephesians 2:1-3, RSV)

In these verses of Ephesians 2, there is a "Prince" who rules over "this world" and has power over "the air." So what is this power? We are told in the very next sentence that he is a spirit. Quite literally spirit (*pneuma,* in Greek) means "power of the air", or *breath*. Let's look a little deeper into this matter.

What is the meaning of "worship"? It is the reverent love and devotion accorded to a deity, an idol, or a sacred object. There are usually ceremonies, prayers, or other religious forms by which this love is expressed. Worship is an ardent devotion, an adoration given to something or someone that ascribes an ultimate "worth-ship", a chiefly British term used as a form of address for magistrates, mayors, and certain other dignitaries.

From strange pontifications from the pulpit, even to Christian songs, bad theology is evident across the board of venues. Bad theology is simply bad teaching not based upon sound Biblical doctrine that is full of error, danger and heresy. Bad theology always leads to bad practice. Many physical and spiritual standards of truth are being adjusted on the fly by religious revisionists who are more interested in validating their thinking than adhering to sound Biblical doctrine.

Each one of us worships something because man was created with a predisposition to worship. What we worship is the key issue that will be discussed in this chapter. Let's break down some of the different forms of worship in every one of our lives.

Music can be as deceptive as it is beautiful. Music is heard 24-hours a day over radio, internet and television stations. There are all types of music from different cultures across the world. One thing that music brings to each human being is a connection to our souls. Our soul consists of our will, our mind and our emotions. Unlike the animals we are also spiritual beings. We are eternal beings and have a desire to worship. Even angels in the Bible worship. Let's take a look at the scriptures.

> *"Son of man, take up a lamentation upon the king of Tyrus, and say unto him, Thus saith the Lord GOD; Thou sealest up the sum, full of wisdom, and perfect in beauty. Thou hast been in Eden the garden of God; every precious stone was thy covering, the sardius, topaz, and the diamond, the beryl, the onyx, and the jasper, the sapphire, the emerald, and the carbuncle, and gold: the workmanship of thy tabrets and of thy pipes was prepared in thee in the day that thou wast created. Thou art the anointed cherub that covereth; and I have set thee so: thou wast upon the holy mountain of God; thou hast walked up and down in the midst of the stones of fire." (Ezekiel 28: 12-14, KJV)*

This is not an earthly king, as the word "cherub" is only used in references to angels.

> *"How art thou fallen from heaven, O Lucifer, son of the morning! How art thou cut down to the ground, which didst weaken the nations! For thou hast said in thine heart, I will ascend into heaven, I will exalt my throne above the stars of God: I will sit also upon the mount of the congregation, in the sides of the north: Yet thou shalt be brought down to hell, to the sides of the pit." (Isaiah 14:12-15, KJV)*

Satan wanted to be God. The Bible tells us in 2nd Corinthians 4:4 that Satan has become the "god of this world"—and Revelation 20:10 tells us that he will be eternally punished for it.

These scriptures indicate that as part of his original creation by God, Lucifer actually had musical instruments built into his spiritual body. Many theologians believe that before he rebelled against the Lord, Lucifer was in charge of the music in heaven and that he was created to worship God. Can you imagine being perfect in beauty and having magnificent instruments built into you to worship our creator? We must remember that some (though not all) music can come from evil sources no matter how lovely, beautiful or pleasing it may sound to the ears. For we know that the devil can masquerade as an angel of light (2 Corinthians 11:14). I believe music has a two-fold purpose: either to glorify God, or to entertain the passions of men. It's as simple as that. As we have seen, music was initially created for God's exclusive glorification up until Satan's rebellion. What he has done with music from that point on becomes a whole other issue.

Before I became a Christ follower, I had quite an impressive collection of music ranging from hard rock to disco, alternative music, mainstream pop, rock, new age to industrial techno music. This was music that I now believe was heavily influenced by Satan. The lyrics to most of these songs are not worth repeating, of which some spoke of and glorified violence, sex, drunkenness, drugs, etc. One day I came across a popular Christian evangelist speaking out about the Satanic influences of music in today's pop-culture. The sermon spoke about how today's ungodly music worms its way into our homes and our cars, ultimately influencing our hearts and minds. There have even been scientific studies proving that music severely influences our psyche, and the outcome of our behavior is contingent upon the type of music to which we choose to listen. It was shortly after this discovery that I was led to rid myself of these types of music. Imagine destroying an investment in hundreds of compact discs!

> *"And many of those who practiced magic brought their books together and began burning them in the sight of everyone; and they counted up the price of them and found it fifty thousand pieces of silver." (Acts 19:19, NASB)*

I believe there is plenty of godly and praiseworthy music worth mentioning that exists within our society, music from artists whose sole purpose is to honor and glorify God with the talent with which the Lord has endowed them. Not all music, even secular music, is inherently evil. Just as Satan has an influence on music, so God has His influence on music as well. It has been a historically proven fact that Christ has been the subject of more songs, music, stories, poetry, prose, screenplays, literature, art, etc. than any other subject in history.

There is "Christian" music that exists promoting wrong scriptural doctrine and teaching. Jesus warned of false teachings and false teachers in the end times over and over again. He said many would come in His name saying they are the Christ. "Christ", meaning "anointed", comes from the Greek verb (*chrio*) meaning to smear or anoint. In Matthew 24 verse 5, Jesus warned us not only of false Christs but of people coming in His name saying they are Christians who are not. Does this apply to Christian music as well? Of course it does! If false teachers come teaching and preaching another doctrine, then the enemy will also use so-called "Christian" music to teach false doctrine!

A famous Pastor in California recently stated an alarming message:

> *"I'll Fly Away," "Changed in the Twinkling of an Eye," "Victory in Jesus," "When We All Get to Heaven," "We Shall See the King," and "I'm Getting Ready to Leave This World," have helped to both reflect and nurture this cherished hope we have in Jesus Christ. We have been pilgrims, passing through this world. But our*

hope has shifted, and this shift has brought con-
sequences. I used to sing all those unscriptural
songs..."This world is not my home, I'm just
passing through; My treasures are laid up away
beyond the blue..." Did you ever sing that one?
I've got news for you. This world is your home.
Forever, according to the Word [of God]...Our
final home is right here on earth.

We have shifted from a God-centered, heavenly expectation to one that is man-centered. In effect, the pastor's message is that "we [the church] must conquer for Christ" before Jesus comes back. The hope has shifted from expecting God to complete our redemption and judge the world in righteousness, to the church rising up in "power and glory" and doing exploits!

This pastor has clearly and unmistakably drawn a theological line in the sand. He has made clear that he rejects the classic Biblical teaching of the church's self-identity as a people on a pilgrimage; a people enduring struggle and overcoming it by faith in a Christ who will one day conquer the world Himself. In essence he has embrace what is called "Kingdom Now" thought, which teaches that Christ cannot come back until the church first is in firm control of all of the social systems of humanity. No matter how appealing it sounds, this is not a Biblical position and it is one that has been used to create rank heresy.

This type of shift from sound Biblical doctrine in Christian music to heresy is clearly evident in the above statement. If the message does not line up with the scriptures, throw it out.

Also, I suggest if the band or singer is associated with any type of church or movement that has any type of strange doctrine or "strange fire" (Leviticus 10:1-2), where they are adding to or taking away from God's Word, stay away from it! Music is a form of preaching with a melody. It is also a form of worship, in song, to God. If we are not careful, we may be supporting bands and singers that not only support heresy in their churches, but also release demonic spirits of deception in their concerts. Some of the music in the charismatic movement even sing of and promote sensual encounters and orgasmic experiences, supposedly with the Holy Spirit. These are incubus and succubus spirits that are being released from the Hindu religion to cause great deception in our churches. Yes...demons can and will attack Christians when we are disobedient to God's commandments and, likewise, demons will also possess, attack, and torment the unbeliever.

The incubi and succubi are demonic forces that sexually visit their victims in the night. The incubus is a "male" demon who attacks and violates woman, and the succubi is a "female" demon who seduces and attacks men. In some cases it's be known that the male incubi demon will visit men for the purpose of sodomy. The succubi also will engage in lesbian attacks upon women. I'm writing about this because many Christians believe that these visitations are nothing more than horrid nightmares. In some cases it seems that the nightmare (which is from the Latin meaning to "*lie upon*") is just that – a bad dream. But occasionally this is nothing to do with bad dreams, but can be an actual demonic visitation. The attacks from these spirits may begin by the victim having sexually arousing dreams, but that's only a vehicle for what comes next.

Here I want to confine the discussion to dreams, and how demons will use these. Basically if a person has a loose mind, addiction to pornography, one that is prone to fantasize, and lacks self-discipline, they may become a target for these powers. Those who have indulged in excessive sexual activity are also likely to experience such visitations.

These, by themselves, are not the only factors that will draw a demon to visit, but also as issues such as occult involvement and un-confessed sexual sin may also determine whether a person is a candidate. Therefore, it's important to guard your dream-life by committing your time of sleep to the Lord.

Some pastors teach that we should have a romantic, lover's relationship with Jesus based on the model of the woman's desire for her lover in Song of Songs. While there may be a parallel at the corporate level of the church, to Christ's love for His body, it could confusingly imply a homosexual eroticism to Christian men to relate to Jesus individually in this way, or confuse an unintended incestuous fixation for Christian women to view Jesus as their brotherly lover. The lyrics of these songs reflect this teaching on what is called in certain circles the "Bridal Paradigm": *"We're lovesick… Your beauty ravishes us, "Kiss me with the kisses of your mouth… No wonder the maidens love you… Let the King take me to His chamber"*. The pursuit of this type of intimacy along with graphically sexu-alized visualization and other New Age techniques can lead a person to spiritual seductions of another spirit altogether. I wonder if we are starting to see *"the working of Satan, with all power, signs and lying wonders,"* (2 Thessalonians. 2: 9) partly as a result of this. We certainly can't assume that just because healings and miracles take place at these churches and concerts that these are necessarily coming from God's Spirit. In fact, I believe according to the scriptures that many signs, wonders and miracles will happen in His name not from the true believers but from wolves that come in practicing wickedness dressed as sheep. Jesus has specifically warned us that these things will also come from Satan. If you do not have a love for the truth, you too will be deceived.

> *"Many will say to Me on that day, 'Lord, Lord, did we not prophesy in Your name, and in Your name cast out demons, and in Your name perform many miracles?' "And then I will declare to them, 'I never knew you; DEPART FROM ME, YOU WHO PRACTICE LAWLESSNESS.' (Matthew 7:22-23, NASB)*

> *"For false Christs and false prophets will rise and show great signs and wonders to deceive, if possible, even the elect," (Matthew 24:24, NKJV)*

> *"do not believe every spirit, but test the spirits, whether they are of God," (1 John 4:1, NKJV)*

There are other types of inspirational music that is also very dangerous. Let's talk about the "new age" music section in our retail stores or on iTunes, CD baby, satellite radio, etc. Inspirational music can sound religious but can produce deadly effects into our lives. The common thread that unites these otherwise diverse forms of New Age music is supposed to be *"feeling"*—listening to them generates a peaceful and uplifting mood. These genres of music use richly spacious melodies to evoke these mood changes, using anything from Tibetan gongs to human chants to synthesized midi loops. They seek an opening of one's spiritual receptivity as well as an altered state of mind that suspends judgment and fixates upon personal experience as the foundation of one's truth.

How dangerous is New Age music? The primary means for conveying spiritual influences through music is words. Since most New Age music is nonverbal, except for song titles, this opportunity rarely exists in other types of music.

When it comes to melodies and rhythms, there is a much greater possibility with music than with lyrics for the original intention to become diffused in the medium. Thus, while the composer may intend to elicit a particular mystical mood, the "non-initiate" listener simply becomes more relaxed. I believe this would be the case with most "inner" harmony New Age music.

After all, even when New Agers are specifically attempting to induce altered states of consciousness through their music, much of their applied theory is based on New Age presuppositions which some Christians would not be inclined to accept. These include belief in the correspondence of particular sound frequencies with more or less mystical levels of consciousness, and an equation of certain relaxed or emotional states with mystical states. Additionally, some New Age melodies are so obviously patterned after familiar mystical or meditative rhythms (e.g., the mystical refrain "om") that their pagan associations are inescapable. Listening to such music for entertainment or relaxation could easily result in someone stumbling. Either the listener or another believer could begin to associate the highest form of spirituality in Eastern mysticism when it is linked to a musical form that seems profound and "spiritual".

> *"Wherein in time past ye walked according to the course of this world, according to the prince of the power of the air, the spirit that now worketh in the children of disobedience." Ephesians 2:2, KJV)*

More Worship

Music is not the only form of worship to the beast or to our God. There are also other forms of worship in our lives. Our obedience to God not only glorifies Him but is also a form of worship to Him. Our disobedience and rebellion, likewise, not only glorifies the devil but also gives sacrifices of worship to him. I can just see the incense of smoke rising across the world giving homage to the enemy of God and his creation by millions of people who live in sin and rebellion. In fact, I believe that every time we sin, and of which we do not repent, we give worship to Satan himself. As Christians we may not verbally do this but in our actions we definitely do.

> *"These people honor me with their lips, but their hearts are far from me." Matthew 15:8 (NIV)*

Jesus speaks about the hearts of men. Men cannot see our hearts but God surely does. He tests the motives of our hearts to see if they are pure. Jesus said:

> *"Are you still lacking in understanding also? Do you not understand that everything that goes into the mouth passes into the stomach, and is eliminated? But the things that proceed out of the mouth come from the heart, and those defile the man. For out of the heart come evil thoughts, murders, adulteries, fornications, thefts, false witness, slanders. These are the things which defile the man; but to eat with unwashed hands does not defile the man." (Matthew 15:16-20, NASB)*

According to Jesus, we can know the heart by what proceeds out of the mouth.

Our mouth is a powerful tool. It is used to praise God or to curse men. When we speak, we are either glorifying God or the devil. *"For by your words you will be justified, and by your words you will be condemned."* (Matthew 12:37, ESV) When you hear a man or woman make light of sin or evil it is a sure sign that will be the path that they will also follow.

The worldly paths of worship have also crept into our churches. Giving to God financially to support your local church, or even giving offerings to ministries to further the spreading of the Gospel, is a form of worship. If, in return, when we demand material possessions from God, we value them more than we honor God. How many times have you heard a television or church preacher promise that if you give your money to them you will receive more money, a house or a car? If you have done this, you have fallen into idolatry. We should never give money to God to purchase any type of blessing. Jesus said:

> *"Listen, my beloved brethren: did not God choose the poor of this world to be rich in faith and heirs of the kingdom which He promised to those who love Him? But you have dishonored the poor man. Is it not the rich who oppress you and personally drag you into court? Do they not blaspheme the fair name by which you have been called?" (James 2:5-7, NASB)*

A person who is deceived by this teaching of material wealth has fallen prey already to the seduction of their own hearts whether knowingly or unknowingly. There is nowhere in scripture that says God wants you to be rich financially. He tells us to be content with what we have (Hebrews 13:5). He even warns us that the rich fall into many temptations (1 Tim 6:9). If we justify that God wants us to have and desire money and possessions it is not the correct interpretation and teaching that we have been receiving. Ask the Holy Spirit to teach and guide you into all truth so that you will not be deceived.

> *"As for you, the anointing which you received from Him abides in you, and you have no need*

for anyone to teach you; but as His anointing teaches you about all things, and is true and is not a lie, and just as it has taught you, you abide in Him." (1 John 2:27, ESV)

True Worshippers

Most Christians are familiar with the verse in John 4:24, where Jesus said we need to worship God in spirit and in truth, but how many of us actually do what it says? Do you know how to worship God in spirit and truth? Are you sure God accepts your current form of worship? Do you worship in accordance with scripture or do you just go along with the crowd? Can you say with confidence, "NO COMPROMISE", about your relationship with Christ Jesus? Are you separating yourself from sin and the things of this world? Friend, we are living in the end times of earth's history and Satan is doing all he can to deceive God's children and cause them to compromise their faith. If, however, we worship God according to the Spirit and the truth of His Word, then we will not be deceived by the evil one.

Worshiping God in spirit means we worship Him from the heart. Do you remember the first and greatest Bible Commandment that Jesus gave? *"And thou shalt love the Lord thy God with all thy heart, and with all thy soul, and with all thy mind, and with all thy strength: this is the first commandment..'* (Mark 12:30, KJV) Most Christians will be happy to quote this Bible verse, but how many of us really do what it says? Just as the Bible verse in John says that we

MUST worship God in spirit and truth, this verse in Mark COMMANDS us to love the Lord God with all our heart, soul, mind and strength. This verse means we must give our all to Him; all our time, all our money and possessions, all of ourselves. Not just some, but ALL. Worshipping God in truth means to worship Him according to His Word in the Bible—"*Sanctify them through thy truth: <u>thy Word is truth</u>.*" (John 17:17, KJV)

Many church denominations are now deciding for themselves how they should worship God rather than abiding by the truth of God's holy Word in the Bible. Let me give you an example. Just recently, the Church of England, in some parts of the UK, has decided to replace hymns with rock songs by the band U2. Instead of explicitly worshiping God by singing good traditional hymns, with words that give glory and honor to God, they will sing secular "rock" songs with vague references to a shadowy and ill-defined spirituality. It is plain to see that as we near the end of time, many churches are wandering further and further from the truth of God. I cannot believe that the Spirit of God is found in that kind of worship; worship blended with worldly music, or anything else worldly for that matter.

We worship God because He created us through and by Jesus Christ, our Lord and Savior. We worship God because He has freed us from the penalty of our sins through the sacrifice of our Lord and Savior, Jesus Christ. We worship God because of the promise of eternal life with Him if we serve Him with all our heart, mind and soul. We worship God because He comforts us in times of distress. We worship God because of His unfailing love for each and every one of us. He loves us with a love that goes far beyond anything we know. Friend, we have an amazing God and He deserves all the glory, honor, praise, and exaltation we can give Him. This is why He wants us to worship Him in spirit and truth and not just in any old way.

For some reason, the majority of the Christian world believes it needs to "keep up with the times", that it needs to be more modern and therefore, needs to bring more worldly things into the worship service to entice more people (especially young people) into their church buildings. Is this in line with scripture? Is this in line with worshipping God in spirit and truth? Does the Bible say we need to keep up to date with the world? Of course not! The Bible actually says that we, as the people of God, need to stay separate from the world. We are in the world but we should not be of the world. If we desire our churches to grow, we should always depend on the Lord to bring that increase. The church should be more concerned with preaching the truth as we devote ourselves to praising Him with all that is within us just as did the early church. *"Praising God, and having favour with all the people. And the Lord added to the church daily such as should be saved."* (Acts 2:47, KJV), and, *"But many who heard the message believed, and the number of men grew to about five thousand."* (Acts 4:4, NIV)
Not by gimmicks or compromise.

"Love not the world, neither the things that are
in the world. If any man love the world, the love

29

of the Father is not in him. For all that is in the world, the lust of the flesh, and the lust of the eyes, and the pride of life, is not of the Father, but is of the world. And the world passeth away, and the lust thereof: but he that doeth the will of God abideth for ever." (1 John 2:15-17, KJV)

"And do not be conformed to this world, but be transformed by the renewing of your mind, that you may prove what is that good and acceptable and perfect will of God." (Romans 12:2, KJV)

Life Lessons Study

1. *What types of music do I listen to?*

2. *What was Satan's position in heaven before he fell?*

3. *Does my music promote any rebellion, lust, drugs, anger, or such types of behavior?*

4. *How does my music make me feel towards myself, God and others around me?*

5. *If Jesus was sitting with me listening to this music, what would He say?*

6. *Do I truly worship God with my life and, if not, what areas can I change to please Him?*

7. *Does my Christian music and it's message line up with sound biblical doctrine?*

8. *What music in my collection is the Lord telling me to remove?*

9. *What does it mean to worship God?*

10. *In what areas of my life am I not worshipping God?*

Chapter 2

In the Prophets...

—⌒⌒✠⌒⌒—

I was invited to lead worship at a local conference one
evening, after which a group of us met for dinner. I
was told I should meet a "prophetess" who is from our area.
I resisted the signs and wonders movement but they told me
that she was the real deal. I met her at a restaurant with a
local pastor and evangelist from the conference. She began
to prophesy to me the names of the people I would meet in
the near future. One of them came to pass within a week. She
showed all of us the shape of a heart that had appeared in the
white of her eye, the outline of which having been formed by
a small vein. The heart shape, she told us, had been there she
said for about a year. She flattered me with her words and
many gifts. I took her with me on two major events and every-
where we went, she would know important names, specific
dates of importance, occupations and the past of each person
with whom she would speak. She would speak to people at
airports, restaurants, and on the street and the first thing
they would ask is if she was a psychic. She, along with other
specific people in a major ministry, told me that I would marry
a particular man. This man also told me the same thing and

told me his mother did as well. This man, as it turned out, was quite perverse sexually; he approached me as a wolf in sheep's clothing. When I confronted her about this she said that, even though he was evil, God was giving me a choice. When I questioned her about her past she told me that she never had renounced her psychic powers when she claimed salvation. She said her abilities were always a gift from God. Behind closed doors her behavior with men was seductive, but in front of me it was always dismissed with an innocent, naïve sounding laugh. She knew parts of God's Word but I realized, at that moment, she was sent as a minister of light from the enemy. I cannot imagine the destruction it would have caused, not only to my spiritual and physical safety, but also to the ministry if the Lord had not been faithful. When I confronted her, she refused to repent of her divination.

The word *psychic* comes from the Greek word *psyche*, which is refers to the human mind and soul. These are people who rely upon soulish and mental impulses that can come primarily from demonic spirits, though not exclusively so. Many so-called "psychics" and false prophets operate out of their own lower carnal and natural perceptions and not all are demonic, but make no mistake: demons do have immense, powerful spiritual influence in the souls and minds of humanity today. There are some whose inspiration for what they say and do is drawn from this natural psychic leading but a true prophet, by contrast, is hearing from the Spirit of God.

The apostle Paul said the "natural" or "psychic" man cannot receive the things of the Spirit of God (1 Corinthians 2:14). A psychic may claim to hear spiritually, and know what will happen in the future, but the difference between a psychic and a true prophet of God is the **source** of the spiritual knowledge. Most psychics have no idea from whom, or where, is the source of their power. They know they possess a "spiritual" gift, and exercise it, but have no understanding of Biblically validated spiritual truth.

A prophet understands that the Bible teaches that, existing in the spiritual realm of creation, are the Triune Godhead, the angelic host of heaven, and familiar spirits—also known as demonic spirits. A prophet knows that only one Spirit, the Holy Spirit, leads to God who is Life—and that all other spirits lead to death. The difference between a prophet and a psychic is that a prophet knows that his source of truth, the voice he follows, is that of God.

Countless numbers of people are being led into deception in the end times. A person may either claim to be a "prophet" or they are deceived by false prophets at an alarming rate. Some of these "prophetic" people operate out of the spiritual energy of psychic powers. There is a very popular notion going around in charismatic church circles today which teach that psychic powers such as clairvoyance and ESP are gifts given to people by God, at their birth, and that when such gifted ones receive Christ they then use those gifts for the purposes God originally intended. There is also a false teaching that has gained popularity which states that people are born with the gifts of the Spirit; a rationale when it is difficult to tell the difference between ungodly psychics and so-called Christian prophets.

When Christians accept the belief that psychic phenomena

is an inborn gift that can be used for either good or for evil, and that the gifts of the Spirit are one and the same, they have fallen into a dangerous snare of deception. This is a rejection of the Bible's teaching on the gifts of the Spirit, demoting them to a natural ability, like singing. The hunger for psychics is the same hunger that these new age God-chasers want to see fostered in the church.

How many times has a so-called prophet been sent into our lives and we believe what they say is from God? There are countless so-called Christian ministries that charge money to give people a so-called "Word" from the Lord.

> ."Tell us," they said, "when will this happen, and what will be the sign of your coming and of the end of the age?" Jesus answered, "Watch out that no one deceives you, for many will come in my name... At that time many will turn away from the faith... and many **false prophets** will appear and deceive many people." (Matthew 24:3-5, 10-11, NIV)

We see here, and in many other places throughout scripture, that "false prophets" will appear. The inability to discern a false prophet from a true prophet will open the way for the deception of *the* False Prophet—the beast "out of the Earth" (Revelation 13:11) who is the end time co-worker of the Antichrist. All the marks of a false prophet should be understood by the body of believers and applied to our daily discernment of who ought to be believed and who ought to be rejected.

*"For every one that useth milk is unskillful in the Word of Righteousness: for he is a babe. But Strong Meat belongeth to them that are of full age, even those who **by reason of use have their senses exercised to discern both good and evil.**" (Hebrews 5:13-14, KJV)*

Our Lord did not excuse the hypocrites for their lack of discerning the "signs of the times" (Matthew 16:3) and neither will He excuse the world for allowing the "False Prophet" to deceive them into worshipping the Antichrist.

Every false prophet will cause you to eventually turn away from the Lord. Pivotal to the concept of identifying false prophets is that a false prophet seeks to turn people away from the Lord Jesus Christ, i.e., *"Let us go after other gods, which thou hast not known, and let us serve them" (Deuteronomy 13:2).* If we understand that our loving obedience to the Word of God is the basis for our certainty that we belong to Him, then we also know that anyone who is clearly in disobedience to the commands of our Lord Jesus Christ is a liar.

"And Moses answered and said, But, behold, they [the Children of Israel] will not believe me, nor hearken unto my voice: for they will say, The LORD hath not appeared unto thee...And it shall come to pass, if they will not believe also these two signs [the rod into a serpent, and the leprous hand], neither hearken unto thy voice, that thou shalt take of the water of the river, and pour it

upon the dry land: and the water which thou takest out of the river shall become blood upon the dry land." (Exodus 4:1, 9, KJV)

"And the sign or the wonder come to pass, whereof he spake unto thee, saying, Let us go after other gods, which thou hast not known, and let us serve them;" (Deuteronomy 13:2, KJV)

We are to not think it strange that even a false prophet can make the "sign or a wonder come to pass" by the supernatural power of Satan. But their "message" will always turn your heart away from God. In the Old Testament, these types of prophets were stoned.

"For there shall arise false Christs, and false prophets, and shall shew great signs and wonders; insomuch that, if it were possible, they shall deceive the very elect." (Matthew 24:24, KJV)

Many false prophets have been sent into my life. A few years ago I attended, for thirteen years, a different church than the one I now attend. There was, at that church, a guest "prophetess" who was leading a three day revival. On one of those nights I stood in the back of the church among two-thousand people. During the service, she was calling out people's sins, secrets, and exposing them to the entire congregation. I was very troubled as I watched and, though everyone was clapping and shouting, a red flag I felt in my spirit would not allow me to participate in approval of her and of what she was doing. At the end of the service she pointed me out to everyone from the stage. She told me to come out into the aisle and she would come to me. She began to lay her hand on my forehead and tell me in front of everyone how my heart was not right with God, that my sin was very deep, and that God would not bless me until I got right with Him. Then she tried to force me to fall backward to the ground. I would not go, so she pushed me and I fell on my behind sitting up on the ground. I heard the claps of the entire congregation and I realized at that moment that they had just come into agreement with her. I was devastated. My mentors, my Pastor, and everyone I knew allowed this to happen, without challenge, though I had been in ministry for many years with an excellent reputation. I cried all the way home and could not believe what occurred in front of thousands of people. That was the last night I would ever attend that church.

Right after that experience, I went to visit another church with a friend who was a part of their altar prayer team. This church broadcasts on television and is one of the largest in the Detroit area. While we were sitting in the front row, my friend said the woman in charge of the prayer team had "a word from the Lord" for me and wanted me to meet her in front of the altar following the service, which I did. She told me to lift my hands and she proceeded to tell me that I use my body to have sex with men and she used to do the same thing before she lost her figure (she was about 350 pounds). She said I had total un-forgiveness in my heart and that I harbored bitterness. I was completely astounded, especially since she was the head intercessory prayer leader of that church. Not only was I shocked, but she was completely wrong. I told my friend, who was a part of her intercessory prayer team, and she completely dismissed it.

I cannot imagine what I would have done if I were a new Christian and these types of things had happened to me. I believe I would have turned away from God and thought Christians were freaks. These people acted out of a lying spirit of divination drawn out of their own twisted souls. Either way, it was a painful personal realization of a carnal religious spirit that can rise up within a person to establish their own traditions and agenda. This is a sinful denial of God's Word and destructive to the unlearned and new babes in Christ

Prophets for today...

"In the past God spoke to our forefathers through the prophets at many times and in various ways, but in these last days he has spoken to us by his Son, whom he appointed heir of all things, and through whom he made the universe." (Hebrews 1:1-2, NIV)

The Age of the Prophets, who were undoubtedly famous men within their own societies, has now past. The great Hebrew prophets could claim an audience before kings and princes and were undoubtedly famous men indeed; men of renown who changed history. Yet scriptures, such as Romans 12:6, 1 Corinthians 12:10 and 14:29-32, show that a gift of prophecy can be expected to be witnessed in the New Covenant Church of God!

It seems quite plain from a consideration of Acts and 1 Corinthians 14:29-32 that the New Testament gift of prophecy is quite different to the Old Testament concept of 'prophet'. The new prophets are expected to be active *within church congregations* and not necessarily famous or renowned beyond that. One of the difficulties for us in understanding the conception of prophet in our day is partly due to the fact that the Greek word, *propheteis*, is really much broader than our English word, 'prophet', which tends to have quite a specific ring. Truthfully, the Greek word can just as easily mean, 'inspired speaker', or 'encouraging speaker', and some of the New Testament references do not necessarily go beyond that. Yet some scriptures obviously speak of 'prophecy' in a predictive sense. Scriptures to consider here are Acts 11:27-30, Acts 13:1-3, Acts 15:32-34 and Acts 21:10-11. Moreover, the Holy Spirit's action of warning Paul and his companions against speaking in Asia had come through a congregationally based prophet (Acts 16:6-7). The reference to the prophetess, Anna (Luke 2:36), does not need to be taken into our consideration of the New Covenant office of prophet since Anna prophesied well before Christ's sacrifice upon the cross making her one of the very last Old Covenant prophets.

A consideration of these scriptures quickly shows that these congregational prophets were just that, that is, they prophesied of conditions which would affect church congregations or leaders. In Acts 11:27-30, Agabus prophesies of a famine that would spread over *'the entire Roman world'*—which would obviously affect Christian congregations in those regions. The text clearly tells us that this occurred *'during the reign of Claudius'* (v. 28).

In Acts 13:1-3, we again see the mention of prophets. This might appear at first to be a looser use of the word 'prophet', but it seems they are only mentioned here because of a message to set apart Paul and Barnabas. (v.2).

When we come to Acts 15:32-34, there is mention of Judas and Silas being prophets. The use here could well denote the definitions of 'encourager' and 'inspirer' as no predictive prophecy is mentioned.*"Judas and Silas, who themselves were prophets, said much to encourage and strengthen the brothers"* (v. 32). In other words, a paraphrased reading of this verse states that this might mean little more than, 'Judas and Silas who, themselves, were very encouraging and inspiring speakers, said much to encourage and strengthen the brothers'.

We now come to Acts 21:10-11. Agabus is here, again, involved. He utters a predictive prophecy regarding Paul which, by the way, probably occurred some 15 years after the occasion of Acts 11:27-30.

We can see that there were, indeed, New Covenant prophets, but they bore little resemblance to the Old Testament Hebrew prophets who had been *national* figures, warning of various *national* calamities which would befall Israel and Judah if the people did not turn from their wicked ways! The New Testament office, however, only appeared concerned with Christian congregational life and with the protection of Christian leaders.

We now need to look more closely at 1 Corinthians 14, which tells us something about the use of both 'tongues' and prophecies in first-century congregational life.

Firstly, a careful consideration of verses 27-33 reveals that confusion was forbidden within the congregation. Two people were never to speak at once! Regarding tongues (which we are not discussing in this chapter), if there was to be no inter-pretation, the one who might wish to speak was to be quiet (v. 28). Corinth was a thriving seaport in which people of several nationalities could be present; it would be natural for some of these people to praise God in their native tongue, but Paul points out that the edification of the *whole* congregation was important. Then the text discusses prophets. Two or three could speak but, again, *never at the same time!-* maintaining orderly conduct without confusion was obviously deemed very important (v. 33). Paul writes that, *"The spirits of prophets are subject to the control of prophets"* (v. 32).

In other words, prophets have no automatic right to go too far or beyond their moment of inspiration! There seems little doubt that this is a looser sense of a prophet than in the sense of Agabus, since whatever a prophet said was to be *evaluated* (v. 29), and presumably such an evaluation would come from the congregation's elder (or, minister). These people were obviously not allowed free reign to say whatever they wanted without evaluation! Paul obviously recognized that prophecy could be a gift, but this is unquestionably a looser sense of prophecy in which a Christian might receive a moment of inspiration, rather than any sense that the early church was simply filled with prophets of the stature of Agabus!

Paul's stern warning against disorderliness and confu-sion obviously shows that reports had reached him of some confusion during meetings at Corinth! Extreme charismatic churches should heed warning! Obviously speaking primarily to those who occasionally spoke in tongues, or uttered prophecies, Paul goes as far as saying, *"If he ignores this, he himself will be ignored"*

(v. 38). Again, these people were obviously not uttering prophecies like Agabus' warning, through the Holy Spirit, that a famine would affect the entire Mediterranean area.

We surely have to conclude that the nature of prophecy found in 1 Corinthians 14 is clearly of a far more inclusive sense (don't forget that the Greek word for prophecy is rather broad), and may be defined as a moment of divinely inspired utterance originating from among the Christian congregation. My own careful consideration of Romans 12:6 and 1 Corinthians 14:29-32 leads me to believe that *'prophesy'*, here, means, 'to speak inspirational/encouraging words in public', deriving from a conception of *'prophet'* which (in these verses) would mean, 'One divinely enabled to speak inspiring, encouraging or revelatory words to others in public'. We would now call this 'the gift of preaching'. It is particularly clear from 1 Corinthians 14:29-32 that Paul felt that these 'prophecies' might emanate from *any* part of the congregation, amounting to even three occasions during a service! People like Agabus, however, whom the Holy Spirit directed to utter predictive warnings to the church, were undoubtedly rare. Again, any careful evaluation of Paul's words in these verses shows that he is not talking about *congregational prophets* of the stature of Agabus! We must ensure that we don't go beyond what the inspired text actually says.

The New Testament does warn of false prophets who have always been around. Consult Acts 13:6-10 and Revelation 2:20. Let's also look at Matthew 7:

> *"Watch out for false prophets. They shall come to you in sheep's clothing, but inwardly they are ferocious wolves. By their fruit you will recognize them." (Matthew 7:15-16, NIV)*

In Acts 2:17-18 we read, *"In the last days, God said, 'I will pour out my Spirit on all people. Your sons and daughters will prophesy, your young men will see visions, and your old men will dream dreams. Even on my servants, both men and women, I will pour out my Spirit in those days, and they will prophesy."* Clearly, since the time of Christ, we have been living in "the last days" and this gift is anything but gone. More than with any other label, however, we must use extreme caution when either demonstrating this gift or receiving it from others, because we are forewarned: *"Dear friends, do not believe everyone who claims to speak by the Spirit. You must test them to see if the spirit they have comes from God. For there are many false prophets in the world..."* (1 John 4:1, NLT)
Some of the signs of a true and authentic prophet (not inclusive) are:

- ***They have received this gift from the Holy Spirit*** (See 1 Corinthians 12:28-29 & Ephesians 4:11). Sometimes, however, God temporarily gifts people to prophesy for a specific purpose when they are not prophets, such as when Saul began prophesying as a sign from God that he would be the next king (see 1 Samuel 10:9-11).

- ***They will always agree with scripture or what the Lord has previously spoken.*** Such was the case in 1 Kings 13 when God told a certain man to deliver a message to King Jeroboam and to leave without eating or drinking in that town. A lying prophet approached him and told him that God said it was okay for him to eat at his house after all. The man believed the prophet and ate with him, which resulted in devastating consequences. The man should have realized the lie and stuck with what God had already told him.

- ***If what they speak is truly from the Lord, it will come true, 100% to the letter.*** "So a prophet who predicts peace must carry the burden of proof. Only when his predictions come true can it be known that he is really from the LORD." (Jeremiah 28:9) Otherwise, he is a false prophet. God always rebuked the false prophets if their prophecy was not 100 % true or if it did not come to pass. You cannot be a prophet with a 65% accuracy and still be called a prophet (Isaiah 44:24-26, Ezekiel 12:25, 1 Thess. 5:20-21). A false prophet can also have their "signs and wonders" come to pass but their message is to turn your heart away from God. This type of prophet, or 'dreamer of dreams' in the Old Testament, was put to death (Deuteronomy 13:1).

- ***Their prophetic words should be confirmed.*** God ALWAYS speaks through His Word. The confirmation should come within the bounds of scripture. Extra Biblical revelation is a dangerous course to take. Many lives are ship-wrecked through this type of encounter even when others confirm the prophecy that was spoken to them.

- ***Their lives will be aimed at godliness.*** Jeremiah 23:14 says, *"And among the prophets of Jerusalem I have seen something horrible: They commit adultery and live a lie. They strengthen the hands of evildoers, so that no one turns from his wickedness. They are all like Sodom to me..."* God cares about hypocrisy among those speaking in His name, and so should you.

- ***They will speak truth in a spirit of humility.*** Many of the prophets in the Bible spoke with authority and bold-ness, but all of them spoke in humility. Jesus was the ultimate example.

- ***They announce sins before promising blessings.*** A blessed life is no good if you're still lost in your sins. God has always had the condition of obedience before blessing. In Lamentations 2:13b-14 we read, *"Your wound is as deep as the sea. Who can heal you? The visions of your prophets were false and worthless; they did not expose your sin to ward off your captivity. The oracles they gave you were false and misleading."* (Also see Jeremiah 23:16-17, 22)

- ***They are offensive to many without seeking to be offending.*** People do not always want to hear the truth;

hence, prophets are not usually popular. Isaiah 30:9-11 says, *"These are rebellious people, deceitful children, children unwilling to listen to the LORD's instruction. They say to the seers, 'See no more visions!' and to the prophets, 'Give us no more visions of what is right! Tell us pleasant things, prophesy illusions. Leave this way, get off this path, and stop confronting us with the Holy One of Israel!'"* (See also Luke 4:24, Acts 7:51-52, 2 Timothy 4:3)

- ***They won't predict "new truths" about end times and their words will not conflict with or go outside the bounds of scripture.*** Revelation 22:18 says, *"If anyone adds anything to what is written here, God will add to that person the plagues described in this book."*

- ***Their gift isn't "one size fits all."*** Consider King David. Acts 2:30 tells us that David was a prophet yet, during his life, you don't find him foretelling events to individuals, like, say, Isaiah or Ezekiel, or displaying special powers like Moses or Elijah. Throughout the Psalms, however, David prophesied of the coming Messiah and His kingdom. So there are different kinds of prophets, and different kinds of messages.

Remember, the gift of prophecy can work out in many different ways. A few examples might be in dreams, special insight either from the Bible or in life situations, direction for future events, declaration of sin, and even just "truth-telling." It can come from many different vessels, according to Acts 2—men, women, the elderly and even children.

One must use extreme caution and "wait it out" to see whether the word is from God, lest we be tricked by a false gift or a false impression.

One warning: Be very careful about speaking for the Lord or interpreting His message! 2 Peter 1:20-21 tells us, *"Above all, you must understand that no prophecy of Scripture came about by the prophet's own interpretation. For prophecy never had its origin in the will of man, but men spoke from God as they were carried along by the Holy Spirit."* (NIV)

It's so easy to receive a word from God and interpret it totally differently from what He meant. It's better to wait to see how He unfolds it, or even if it's from Him. Even after the prophets of the Old Testament, no one had a clue about what the Messianic prophecies meant until after Jesus' death—and even then many still never understood it (also see Jeremiah 23:31-32).

There are many in the Church today claiming "new revelations". There is no new revelation than what has been written in the context of scripture. If we decide to pull scripture out context, it opens the individual up to deception and seducing spirits. Anything God reveals will stay within the bounds of the true context of scripture and its intended meaning in relation to your circumstance. Many teachers are pulling phrases out of the Bible from their proper context and false prophets are tickling the ears of the gullible.

As you can see, determining authentic prophecy is very serious business to God. One can never be too careful.

Life Lessons Study

1. *What is the difference between a prophet and prophesying?*

2. *What is the meaning of Bible prophecy?*

3. *What are some of the differences between a psychic and a prophet?*

4. *Have you ever had someone say to you that something they said was from God, but was not?*

5. *When someone has prophesied to you, how do you test it to know whether it is from God?*

6. *Who are some of the prophets in the Old Testament?*

7. *What type of accountability should a prophet have in the church?*

8. *What should you do when someone comes to you as a prophet and says lies about you?*

9. *Was there ever a time in the Bible when there were lying prophets?*

10. *What is the difference between the prophets of the Old and New Testament?*

Chapter 3

In Media...

O n a beautiful Friday afternoon, I was laying on my couch taking a nap. After two hours, I awoke from my peaceful sleep and turned to look at the television. There was an X-rated movie playing. I was in total disbelief, especially since I only have the Family Channel Package from my cable company. A part of me was so angry because I love the Lord and another part of me was curious and being pulled in to see what was on the screen. I allowed myself to watch for a few seconds and I was disgusted that I even allowed that. I had been delivered for 23 years from pornography addiction and I had just gotten back from ministering and traveling across the United States. I later learned that the cable station had a free movie package for the weekend and it popped up while I had fallen asleep watching Christian television. I felt sick to my stomach and disgusted at the same time. I thought to myself, I can't imagine what others go through in secret when no one is watching behind closed doors. I experienced the filth and defilement against my mind and spirit almost instantaneously.

"Mass media" are various types of media forms designed to reach the largest audience possible. They include television, movies, radio, newspapers, magazines, books, records, video games and the internet. Many studies have been conducted in the past century to measure the effects of mass media on the population in order to discover the best techniques to influence it. From those studies, emerged the Science of Communications, which is used in marketing, public relations and politics. Mass communication is a necessary tool to insure the functionality of a large democracy; it is also a necessary tool for a dictatorship to impose authoritarian control. It all depends on its usage.

The term "Illuminati" is often used to describe a small, elite group, covertly ruling the masses. Although the term sounds quite caricatured and conspiratorial, it is an apt description of the elite's affinities with secret societies and occult knowledge. I personally do not like using the term "conspiracy theory", however, to describe what is happening in the mass media. If all the facts concerning the elitist nature of the industry are readily available to the public, can it still be considered a "conspiracy theory?"

The notion of *escapism* is even more relevant today with advent of online video games, 3D movies and home theaters. The masses, constantly seeking state-of-the-art entertainment, will resort to high-budget products that can only be produced by the biggest media corporations of the world. These products contain carefully calculated messages and symbols which are nothing more, and nothing less, than entertaining propaganda; an agenda of indoctrination meant to influence and condition those who immerse themselves in such products. The public have been trained to LOVE its propaganda to the extent that it spends its hard-earned money to be exposed to it. Propaganda is no longer only used in a politically coercive or authoritarian sense, as found in dictatorships, it has become the driving force of entertainment and pleasure meant to attract, engage, and retain an audience that will clamor for more.

Television may be an effective tranquilizer for noisy or arguing children, but the temporary "peace" it brings can have long-range side-effects as children begin to accept what TV presents as morally right and true reality.

In movies and television there are numerous incidents of verbal aggression, offensive language, problematic behaviors, the paranormal, witchcraft, disrespect for authority, and sexual content. "Respect for the needs of children" and "respect for the American home" have become completely outdated. This powerful influence has corrupted American morals to a degree unimaginable.

The television set indeed hypnotizes and silences everybody in a room when it is on. Once this kind of thing is allowed to happen, the character of a home can actually change. When communication falters, a social vacuum is created; the home is only a place of residence. In it, each person is still alone, isolated, centered on self. The spirit of sharing, of mutual activity and love and help—all the things a family should be—are lost or weakened.

> *"Guard you heart above all else, for it determines the course of your life." (Proverbs 4:23, NLV)*

Research confirms the common-sense assumption that we tend to imitate what we frequently see. This applies to violence as well as generosity. If watching violence leads to violence, and watching generosity leads to generosity, then what are the results of watching the numerous un-Christian ways of thinking and acting that television presents? Is there a connection between television's portrayal of daily relationships, family life, and youth and the noticeable changes in society regarding the decline of honor, the breakdown of family ties, and the glorification of youth?

Television, as well as the other mass media, subtly but surely molds our attitudes and world views. Behind television characters' actions and attitudes there are underlying assumptions about life. Television communicates a loosely coherent world view which makes certain ways of thinking and certain aspects of reality prominent and others absolute. It's the ultimate expression of unreality meant to actually control all reality.

Some are ignored while others are made relative. This is done without Christian perspective. The media world of fact and fiction considers right and wrong in humanistic terms, never in terms of God's Kingdom and His love for the world. It defines freedom in material and political terms, rather than as the liberty from the domination of sin and evil. It insists on knowing only the natural world while ignoring the supernatural or spiritual.

In the long run, television's success in developing un-Christian world views may be more crucial than its immediate impact on behavior and attitude. The basic perspectives on life we draw from the media dominated society around us will often determine what kinds of things we will or will not do.

This conflict between world views becomes clearest when television looks directly at Christianity. In their interviews with

Christian leaders, secular networks consistently emphasize the importance of questions about divorce, materialism, sexual perversion and tax evasion. These are certainly important issues, but this tightly focused television coverage implies that these are the only crucial questions facing Christianity today. They are not. Other issues, such as the role of the Bible in the church, spiritual renewal and evangelism, the life of obedience, and the persecution of the church are also very important, but are generally ignored by the media, probably because they deal with things that are spiritual and supernatural. Scandal, controversy and catching Christians in hypocrisy are a far more attractive lure for programmers to pursue.

The world of television is a world in which Christians are dim-witted, dishonest, or dangerous. For someone taking cues from television, as many do, a Christian individual is not someone to be emulated. There are in real life, undoubtedly, those who profess to be Christian and fall into one of the these categories, but hopefully our good example should make it not only difficult for these portrayals to continue, but easy for a another type to be presented - that of a real Christian, showing a strong but humble witness.

Given the effect on behavior, attitude, and perspective that television has, let us look at the quality or clarity this effect brings with it. Gerbner and Gross, from the University of Pennsylvania, have discovered that heavy television viewers have opinions about the world that differ from factual reality. They see the world as having more professionals, athletes, entertainers, and detectives than it really has. They think society is more affluent than it really is. They see the world as more dangerous than it is, and as a result, are more fearful than light viewers or non-viewers. If this pattern is true, what will be their thinking about how [the] real God cares for people, how wrong sin is, how important genuine life with Christ is, and how to deal with difficulties, triumphs, and failures?

Now more than ever, we are seeing the occult and occult symbolisms increase in our mass media. This should not come as a surprise as the term "occult" literally means "hidden". It also means, "reserved to those in the know", as it is only communicated to those who are deemed worthy of the knowledge. It is not taught in schools, nor is it discussed in the media, whether the general population truly believes in the hidden spiritual world. The enemy's agenda is to desensitize the population to evil spirits, murder, violence, incest, adultery, homosexuality, drugs, the occult, etc.

Occult knowledge is considered normal in occult circles. It is considered timeless and sacred. There is a long tradition of hermetic and occult knowledge being taught through secret societies originating from ancient Egyptians, to Eastern Mystics, to the Knights Templar, to modern day Freemasons. Even if the nature and the depth of this knowledge was modified and altered throughout the centuries mystery schools kept their main features—which are highly symbolic, ritualistic and metaphysical. Occult symbols are now being placed in movies, video games, on television, in music, the internet, and in ad campaigns.

We live in an age when many of us feel as if we are swimming in a sea of information. From broadcast media to cell phones to ubiquitous internet access, we are assailed with more information than we can possibly absorb. On the internet alone we are asked to deal with social networking, blogs, news feeds, forwarded emails, spam, movies on demand and, not to mention, our compulsion to Google any topic that crosses our mind.

One response to this deluge of information is to despair of ever discerning truth in the midst of so many counter claims. After all, what standard can I use to compare competing truth claims? If one medical doctor promotes eating fish daily and another doctor says it is dangerous due to high mercury levels, how can I discern the truth? I may be tempted to retreat into a postmodern mindset, creating my own personal, relative truth that works for me while affirming that others may need to create a different truth which works better for them.

As a Christian, however, I know that there is absolute truth. I may not have full awareness of truth, but it does exist regardless of my lack of knowledge or understanding. Absolute truth is reality as seen from God's perspective, lived out through the person of Jesus Christ and recorded for us in the Holy Bible. When I study the Bible, I find that I am not to be tossed about by all of this competing information, but rather I am to be grounded in the truth, and to speak the truth in love. If I am responsible for speaking truth then God must have equipped me with the ability to discern truth from falsehood.

> *"See to it that no one takes you captive through philosophy and empty deception, according to the tradition of men, according to the elementary principles of the world, rather than according to Christ" (Colossians 2:8, NASB)*

In Christianity...

Whether you watch a televangelist, read Christian books or audio sermons, or faith-based radio programs, deception lurks even within so-called Christian media. A good number of the Christian leadership have been caught in corruption, hypocrisy and lies; deceiving us, and much worse, trying to deceive God himself. Christian television has a mass appeal that reaches an immense number of people, many of whom have only this as their source of information about Christianity. In fact, Billy Graham said that he could reach more people in just one night on television than the Apostle Paul in all of his life. Christian television and televangelism are, in effect, the main, if not the only, representations of Christianity that many people have today. Sadly, many false teachings, distorted information, false ideas, or bad images will be the only reference of Christianity for society and the world at large.

Televangelism has become a business, where preachers work toward better ratings and more donations. They take the scriptures out of context to manipulate people to give, often beyond their means. It is a multi-billion dollar business that preys on the elderly (mostly women), the poor, the biblically illiterate, and the desperate—all in the name of God. I'm not talking about just a handful of television preachers, but most of them. One reason is that there is no accountability for televangelists. If you sent money to any of them, you most likely helped that particular preacher to pay for his jet or his mansion.

"For you know the grace of our Lord Jesus Christ, that, though he was rich, yet for your sakes he became poor, that you through his poverty might be rich." (2 Corinthians 8:9, ESV)

The lavish lifestyle of these televangelists does not reflect in any way the sacrificial life that Jesus and his disciples lived. Incredibly, some television preachers actually claim that Jesus was rich, and there is a wide audience who believe that and anything else that they say. Those people are fooled simply because they do not know the Bible. If they did, no preacher could lie to them because they would immediately realize that those teachings contradict what the Bible says. The Bible repeatedly warns people about all these false teachers, though not even that is a guarantee, since people can be so easily blinded to the truth. What the people reflect is the state of today's society and of the Christian religion, and worst of all, it reflects their own hearts. What I find particularly shocking is how little mainstream Christianity has done to unmask and fight these televangelists.

If Jesus Christ were, as some contend, a mere man, in what sense could he be said to be rich? His family was poor in Bethlehem; his parents were also very poor; he himself never possessed any property among men from the stable to the cross; nor did he have anything at his death. In what way could the poverty of one man make a multitude rich? In Matthew 6:19-21, Jesus said, *"Do not store up for yourselves treasures on earth, where moth and rust destroy, and where thieves break in and steal...But store up for yourselves treasures in heaven, where neither moth nor rust destroys, and where thieves do not break in or steal; for where your treasure is, there your heart will be also."* (NIV)

The biggest reason for people being misled is that the Christian religion has created a system of performers, in the form of clergy and preachers, and a passive audience warming the pews. This audience does not take an active role in searching for truth, learning the Bible, or asking God to guide them, but instead rely on others to show them the way. We should seek, rather, to maintain a direct, undistorted relationship with God totally discarding intermediaries. We should study the Bible with the power of His Spirit as our Teacher (John 14:26) as well using logic and reason to understand what God is trying to say. Trust God, not man.

Televangelists hold to Word-Faith beliefs that are both blasphemous and heretical. Faith preachers say, "Demand what you want by faith and you will receive it!" Moreover, they hold that Christ provided for physical healing at the cross. So not only are Christians saved from sin, they are promised a healthy life! You ask, "Is what they teach biblical?" It is not. Still, Faith teachers contend that their "enlightened" view of the Bible is the gospel truth. Millions blindly adopt their pseudo-spirituality as cutting edge "present truth." Still, some have not yet bowed the knee to these idolatrous beliefs. Read some of the blogs and you will discover that many within the body of Christ find the radical beliefs and practices of the false prophets in the Charismatic movement deeply disturbing.

Jesus did not mince words with this warning:

"Watch out for false prophets. They come to you in sheep's clothing, but inwardly they are ferocious wolves" (Matthew 7:15, NIV)

"Unlike so many, we do not peddle the word of God for profit. On the contrary, in Christ we speak before God with sincerity, like men sent from God." (2 Corinthians 2:17, NIV)

"Many will follow their evil teaching and shameful immorality. And because of these teachers, the way of truth will be slandered. In their greed they will make up clever lies to get hold of your money. But God condemned them long ago, and their destruction will not be delayed." (2 Peter 2:2-3, NLT)

Many televangelists manipulate people to part with their money with the promise that the blessing would be poured out in only two minutes. That's right. Folks had only two minutes to receive God's "exceptional blessing." Credit-card machines were at the ready to accommodate those who were convinced that the "anointing" was flowing through to them. Pay God for a blessing? Leave it to a con-artist to come up with something that preposterous.

If this kind of mind-manipulation weren't such a serious issue in the church, it would be laughable, but it makes you want to cry, and even though people have been warned about televangelists, they continue to contribute to their ministries!

> *"No one can serve two masters. Either he will hate the one and love the other, or he will be devoted to the one and despise the other. You cannot serve both God and Money." (Matthew 6:24, NIV)*

Certainly the Apostle Paul's life would have gone much more smoothly had he been the CEO of a tent company instead of a humble tentmaker. As an itinerant preacher having money would have afforded him first-class accommodations on luxury sailing vessels, however, God did not open up the vault in the "Bank of Heaven", or even grant healing, for his beloved apostles. To Paul he said, *"My grace is sufficient for you, for my power is made perfect in weakness. Therefore I will boast all the more gladly about my weaknesses, so that Christ's power may rest on me"* (2 Corinthians 12:9, NIV). This is authentic Christianity!

I do not believe it is a sin to be rich, but when you use manipulative tactics, twisting God's Word for gain, as in "prosperity gospel" preaching, it becomes utterly detestable.

> *"For such are false apostles, deceitful workers, transforming themselves into the apostles of Christ. And no marvel; for Satan himself is transformed into an angel of light. Therefore it is no great thing if his ministers also be transformed as the ministers of righteousness; whose end shall be according to their works."*
> *(2 Corinthians 11:13-15, KJV)*

Christianity began as a personal relationship with Jesus Christ. When it went to Athens, it became a philosophy. When it went to Rome, it became an organization. When it spread throughout Europe, it became a culture. When it came to America, it became a business.

What is Truth?

Clearly, the Bible teaches us that Satan and the world system are out to take us captive and make us ineffective in our Christian lives by deceiving us into conforming to a perverted view of truth. Every successful con begins with an attempt to validate the trustworthiness of the con-man.

The most dangerous sources of information are those that occupy positions of trust. Consequently, it should come as no surprise that the mechanisms we turn to for factual information or truth are oftentimes the biggest sources of misinformation. In our society, we look to the news media, academia, government and the arts to provide information and perspective to understand reality or truth. As Christians, we need to approach these sources of information with a degree of caution to avoid being taken captive by their distorted worldview.

In what follows, we will focus on how to approach information we receive from the news media (e.g., newspapers, magazines, television, internet news, and blogs). As recognized by the First Amendment of the Bill of Rights, we need the press to be free to provide news and commentary as they see them without fear of retribution. The press, however, can also wield a dangerous amount of power when left unbalanced.

If we are not to be taken captive by the philosophies of a godless world, it is important for us to be on the lookout for biased, agenda-driven reporting. Too many times Christians have been either unaware of the biased message or unconcerned about its impact. Looking back at the social and spiritual changes in our country over the last fifty years, we can see how this lack of awareness and concern have contributed to the emergence of dominant views on morality and religion that are counter to a Biblical worldview.

The Bible instructs us to be on our guard. Let's look as some things we should be doing to proclaim truth in a world filled with misinformation.

Some people suggest that truth is of secondary importance in the work of Christ. According to this view, we should focus on grace and relationship rather than on doctrine and not be concerned if people profess faith in a perception of Jesus that is not consistent with the Biblical record. On the contrary, the Bible is clear that grace and truth are both indispensable parts of the Gospel. Consider three passages from scripture:

> • Paul tells us that "God desires all men to be saved and to come to the knowledge of *the truth*" (1 Timothy 2:4).

> • Jesus explains to Pilate, "For this I have been born and for this I have come into the world, to testify to *the truth*" (John 18:37).

> • In his gospel, John proclaims, "The law was given through Moses, grace and *truth* were realized through Jesus Christ" (John 1:17).

The first step we should take is to know what the Bible teaches and allow the Holy Spirit to use the scripture to bring discernment. As the letter to the Hebrews tell us,

> *"For the word of God is living and active and sharper than any two-edged sword, and piercing as far as the division of soul and spirit, of both joints and marrow, and able to judge the thoughts and intentions of the heart." (Hebrews 4:12-13, NASB)*

Secondly, we need to be alert for warning signs of misinformation. When we recognize the need for discernment, begin by asking God for wisdom in looking for and applying the truth:

> *"But if any of you lacks wisdom, let him ask of God, who gives to all men generously and without reproach, and it will be given to him." (James 1:5-6, NASB)*

Once you have done your research go back to the Bible. God has the only perspective that cannot be deceived by the schemes of the world. Compare your conclusions with scripture and ask the Holy Spirit to lead you into truth. When the facts are not clear, you will not go wrong by being biased in favor of a Biblical worldview. Remember how David delighted in God's Word, saying, *"Your word is a lamp to my feet and a light to my path."* (Psalm 119:10)

Finally, share what you have uncovered with others. Don't let others you know be deceived. Follow the command to speak the truth in love. If you have done some research that others need to know, you may want to look for a venue to share it with a broader audience.

Proper use of the television set, like proper use of any modern convenience, depends on the entire range of values and personal circumstances of the viewers themselves. It cannot be simply dictated by someone outside the family. In the Christian home, family members can help each other to recognize that turning to God, their commitment to Christ, prayer, spiritual growth, and genuine involvement in their local church enables them to face and solve this, or any other issue. Just as with bed-time hours, table manners, and household chores, guidelines must be set up and parents must set a good example. Carefully select programs that will be interesting and informative to the whole family. Do this ahead of time to eliminate random, spontaneous selection. Don't rely on the television set as a diversion too often, as it will become habitual. Don't let younger children turn on the television without permission.

After watching a program, discuss what was seen with the family. Encourage Christian discernment by asking whether or not the show would have been pleasing to God. Show your children that they have a right and a duty to evaluate, not just passively accept, what television offers them. Teach them their standards are those of Jesus Christ and His church, and this should be in every other aspect of their lives. Remember, deception may create detours in our lives, but truth will always be truth and will win out in the end.

"So Jesus was saying to those Jews who had believed in Him, 'If you continue in my word, then you are truly disciples of mine; and you will know the truth, and the truth will make you free.'" (John 8:31-32, NASB)

"Jesus answered,'I am the way and the truth and the life. No one comes to the Father except through me.'" (John 14:6, NIV)

Life Lessons Study

1. *What programs do I watch on television that I know grieve the Holy Spirit?*

2. *When I go to a movie at the theaters, how do I know what offends God?*

3. *Do I have any movies in my house that promote witchcraft, false religion, adultery, lust, etc. Which ones?*

4. *How many hours do I spend in media entertainment in a given week?*

5. *Which movies have I seen that I know are not pleasing to God?*

6. *Should I believe everything that I hear on the news? Explain:*

7. *Who controls the secular media and why?*

8. *Does Christian television always teach what is doctrinally sound?*

9. *Which television preachers have turned you off and why?*

10. *How should we test what we hear on Christian television and secular television to know if it is a deceptive spiritual and emotional teaching?*

Chapter 4

In Unity…

—⟨⟨∘⟩✝⟨∘⟩⟩—

*O*ne afternoon in Charlotte, North Carolina, while sitting in an office while waiting for a meeting, I began speaking with a woman and during our conversation I found out that she was a Christian. I became so excited especially since I had just accepted Jesus as my Lord and Savior. I began to share my testimony and while I was talking she asked me if I had heard of the "Jesus March" that was happening in the city. I told her I had never heard of it. She invited me to attend. I asked her who had put it together and she said that a multitude of churches in the area were getting together and marching for Jesus. She said it was a joint effort and that Catholics, along with other religions, were also coming so we could all march for Jesus. I had only been a Christian a few months but I knew something was wrong with this. I began to wonder how other religions could march when the Jesus that we believed in was far different from the Jesus in whom they believed. I never went to the march but I was quite disturbed for a long time that unity was sought at the expense of sound biblical doctrine. I knew this was not true unity but an acceptance of all religions. When I *questioned her along these lines, she really tried to convince me that this was of God and she became quite agitated that I would even question this event. She said it would bring peace among the diverse religions and, as a Christian, I should support it.*

The one world religion described in Revelation 17:1-18 as "the great harlot" will play a major role in the last day cultural scenario that the Bible prophetically reveals. The term "harlot" is used throughout many of the Old Testament's prophetic passages as a metaphor for false religion. The actual identity and makeup of the religion has been debated for centuries and has resulted in a number of different views among Bible commentators and theologians around the world. There is no doubt that some sort of one world religion that will be led by a literal false prophet will be a part of the end times, perhaps made up of a number of different religions, sects and -isms that are around today.

Revelation 17:1-18 gives us several characteristics of the one world religion. The false religion will dominate all the "peoples and multitudes and nations and tongues" of the earth meaning that it will have universal authority, no doubt, given by the Antichrist who rules the world at that time. Verses 2-3 describe the harlot as committing adultery with the "kings of the earth" referring to the false religion's influence among the world's rulers and influential people. The reference to being drunk with the wine of her adulteries may refer to those who are drunk with the power they receive from worshiping the false god of the false religion. Satan frequently ensnares those whose lust for power drives them away from the worship of the true and living God. The alliances forged by the false religion will unite church and state as never before.

Unity must never be confused with uniformity. There is great emphasis in the church today on uniting professing Christians of all denominations and beliefs. The message is that we're not so different after all; we can work together. Setting aside theological differences, we can help each other in the things we all agree upon. That effort is commonly referred to as "ecumenism," which is defined as *"the organized attempt to bring about the cooperation and unity of all believers in Christ."* Some Christians subvert the Gospel of salvation into a gospel promising world peace through ecumenism, the world-wide unity of all religions. False religious leaders promise that if we reconcile our religious differences and unite with false religions, this will bring peace on earth. Of course, "reconcile our religious differences" really means we must back down and bow down to other gods by repeating the devil's creed: *All religions are equal. We all worship the same god. The equality and brotherhood of man is what we must unite behind.*

Some Christians preach that Jesus' mission was to bring peace on earth—but Jesus never preached world peace and unity. In fact, Jesus declared that standing for His Truth would divide families and nations.

> *"Think not that I am come to send peace on earth: I came not to send peace, but a sword. For I am come to set a man at variance against his father, and the daughter against her mother, and the daughter in law against her mother in*

law. And a man's foes shall be they of his own household." (Matthew 10:34-37, KJV)

There are no moral absolutes in the New Age ecumenical worldview; therefore, it claims to have a spiritual tolerance for all "truth systems" which it calls "harmonization." There is an obvious problem with this notion. To say that there are no moral absolutes establishes a moral absolute, making New Age thought fatally self-contradictory. Similarly, if morality is relative, then stealing may sometimes be right, along with lying, adultery, cheating, etc. Living in a world of moral relativism would not bring a promising future. Logic follows that if reality and truth are relative, then driving a car would be difficult. After all, if one New Ager thinks the traffic light is red and another thinks it's green, when they collide, their differing realities will come crashing down on them. That is something most interesting about New Agers; they don't live what they believe. To claim that we should love everyone while others may desire not to do so are personal choices that should be tolerated, as well as accept that worship of Jesus, as God the Son, alone is just as valid as the worship of the multiple gods of Hinduism!

That is because in reality, New Age thinking—a western form of an Eastern philosophical mindset that embraces contradiction and confusion—doesn't work logically within a framework of actual harmony. While New Age thought **does** espouse honesty, integrity, love, and world peace, it just wants to do it without any reference to the binding Biblical commands of the One True God. It wants to do so on its own relativistic terms, not His terms. When it takes Christian form, it appears beautiful and noble, while hiding behind a cloak of apostasy which too many people never see. Here is an example of a "Unity" church promoting this new age theology:

> *We welcome **all** people into our spiritual family, without any requirement that you give up other spiritual paths, and without regard to your gender, race, politics, sexual orientation, age, dress, hair color, or any of the other artificial barriers to seeing our Oneness. We are all children of God; all one family. Jesus taught an uncompromisingly spiritual gospel centered on **love, acceptance, tolerance, and compassion**. We choose to work to overcome all forms of injustice and bigotry in the world and in our own thoughts and hearts. Because we are all still learning, we learn to forgive each other and ourselves, recognizing that each human being is in process. We look for the **spiritual truth** beyond ego-centered appearances. Every interaction, indeed every moment of our lives, is a lesson; an **opportunity for growth** and spiritual practice. How can I transform this moment? Challenges can be our greatest lessons; "difficult" people, our greatest teachers. We encourage each person to find their "bliss" - to express and share their own unique gifts and talents through **service**, an important part of the path of spiritual growth.*

The above statement promotes tolerance and believes that

there is no absolute truth. Most people who are not true Christians believe that there are many paths that lead to God and you just have to find the path that is best for you.

Compromising the Truth

The undiluted preaching from God's Word and an authoritative stand on truth seem to be on the decline. What we're seeing instead is a broadening of the gospel, a redefining of what it means to be a Christian, and a growing emphasis on inclusion and tolerance of those that do not hold to the Biblical doctrine of Christ. Ecumenism has come to mean "reducing all elements of faith to the lowest common denominator. God's Word is neglected, experience is valued above truth, a false and selfish "faith" is promoted, and sound doctrine and correction are despised as "divisive" and "unloving."

While ignoring the scriptures, numerous evangelical leaders today claim that a concern for doctrine causes division and therefore should be avoided for the sake of love and unity among the brethren. The scriptures, however, couldn't be more specific in their opposition to such a teaching.

> *"Now I beseech you, brethren, mark them which cause divisions and offences contrary to the doctrine which ye have learned; and avoid them. For they that are such serve not our Lord Jesus Christ, but their own belly; and by good words and fair speeches deceive the hearts of the simple."*
> *(Romans 16:17-18, KJV)*

Divisions are created by teachings that are contrary to sound doctrine. For this reason, Christendom, or Christianized culture itself, has perverted Christianity for two millennia into a massive global exercise of toleration of doctrinal division – but at what cost? Unity in the faith is impossible without the doctrine of Christ. Without such a foundation we have no basis for the faith, for the Gospel, for knowing Jesus, or for knowing anything pertinent to the truth.

> *"Whosoever transgresseth, and abideth not in the doctrine of Christ, hath not God. He that abideth in the doctrine of Christ, he hath both the Father and the Son." (2 John 1:9, KJV)*

The glittering terminology of ecumenism is seen, on close examination, to be as hollow as a soap bubble and just as slippery and hard to hold onto. Where is the "common ground" between belief and unbelief? A believer cannot ignore the "major theological differences" between him and an unbeliever. Instead, he should be cutting through those differences with the sword of the Word to establish foundational truth, so as to equip the body of Christ to win unbelievers to the lordship of Jesus Christ.

I cannot agree to ignore an unbeliever's condition without, by that very act, compromising my beliefs. For my beliefs include the "Great Commission", which requires me to tell the world of the Gospel of Jesus. Scripture has much to say about Christian unity. At its most fundamental level all true believers are united in Christ by a spiritual union with Him; the result of the work of the Spirit in our hearts through faith in the truth of the Gospel. The scriptures command us NOT to create spiritual unity, but to build upon the unity which already exists in Christ through the bond of the Spirit (Galatians 4:6) by acts of love and service in the context of local churches (e.g., John 17:22-23; Romans 12:4-5; Ephesians 4:3-6,13; Colossians 3:13-15). Because Christian unity comes through faith it involves a unity in truth. That is why the scriptures constantly urge us to preserve our unity by upholding the knowledge of the truth - in both doctrine and deed (John 8:31-32). Growth in knowledge and understanding of the Gospel is seen as a key for expressing our unity. Indeed, love is even defined in terms of obedience to the truth of the Word (e.g., John 14:15, 21, 23-24; 1 John 2:3-6). When our agreement in the truth is great, then visible unity and our spiritual growth increases as well. This is why we are urged to seek the ideal of "one mind" despite remaining differences (1 Corinthians 1:10; 2 Corinthians 13:11; Ephesians 4:13).

If we are united through the truth of the Gospel applied to our hearts by the Spirit it follows that division stems from error or heresy—a denial of truth in teaching or practice. This is indeed the clear teaching of scripture. We are warned to test everything in order that our unity be preserved (Romans 16:17-18; Titus 1:9-11; 1 John 4:1). On minor matters on which the scriptures do not directly speak, there is room for difference within our fundamental unity (1 Corinthians 11:19; Romans 14). However, all teaching is to be subject to the test of the Word. Where it falls short, people are to be lovingly corrected through the discipline and intervention of the church. Where people deny the faith by heresy or immorality, the scriptures insist that we separate from them, NOT because we are causing division but in order to pre-serve the spiritual unity which they deny. It is always error that divides. Truth unites. This is why Evangelicals cannot 'unite' with Roman Catholicism, for the latter still denies the central issues of the Biblical Gospel and expounds a unity alien to the Gospel. This is also why the "Word of Faith" movement, with its denials of Biblical atonement and carnal preoccupation with worldly gain must also be rejected.

Another common view errs in thinking that "unity" is expressed through "being tolerant"—simply by not disagreeing with anyone's positions or beliefs. Based upon this view, anyone who seeks to challenge or test someone else (at least publicly) is breaking the unity of the body of Christ. This is a sad and fragile unity indeed! It is completely incompatible with the kind of scriptural unity we've discussed, as the apostles were willing to publicly rebuke and correct individuals and churches, and urged the churches to do likewise, in light of the Word (e.g., 1 Corinthians 5; Titus 1:9-11; 2 Peter 2). Scriptural unity is not a superficial tolerance but a deep spiritual bond based on Biblical truth and committed to upholding that truth. This means that, at times, a Christian or group may have to be lovingly challenged if they are denying (in doctrine or deed) the unity they profess to have with us (as in warnings in the letters to the churches in Revelation 2-3, 1 John 2:19).

If true division is to separate from error for the sake of the truth, then false division is to embrace and promote error at the expense of truth and thereby divide the body of Christ. It is false teaching and practice that divides churches. False teaching ultimately arises from reading scripture in light of extra-Biblical traditions, experience or reason. This is why the scriptures urge us to test these things (1 John 4:1). The severest warnings of scripture are directed toward those who so divide Christ's body (e.g., Matthew 18:6; Hebrews 6:4-6; 10:25-31; 2 Peter 2).

Ministers and teachers crying "Unity! Unity!" the loudest, who accuse others of "dividing the body" by daring to question their teachings or practices, are often the very ones who are dividing the body of Christ by the introduction of new and unbiblical teachings and practices. We have a responsibility to preserve our unity by testing all things according to His Word (including ourselves) as found in 2 Corinthians 13:5: *"Examine yourselves, whether ye be in the faith; prove your own selves..."* (KJV)

We are called to express unity through our obedience to the truth, especially the central and saving truths of the Gospel by which we are saved. It goes without saying that, in carrying out such a task, we are to do it with a humble attitude of loving concern for the cause of Christ and His people.

Jesus never preached a Gospel urging unity with false religions to usher in world peace. And Jesus never stopped preaching the truth because it offended the hypocritical scribes and Pharisees, hardhearted Jews, infidels and the multitudes— for He, himself, was the complete embodiment of truth itself (John 14:6). Today, when there are so many who are professing religion, is it any wonder that some of the deepest truths in the Bible—repentance, faith, holiness, etc.—are also some of the greatest objects of debate in the church. It must be said that those who truly want to know God's views on these great pillars of Christian doctrine will appear to be divisive—and rightly so in an age when the great gospel message of salvation can be reduced to a sugar-coated, spiritual bakery item such as, "God loves you and has a wonderful plan for your life", or "your best life is now!"

The truth offends those who don't want to hear it, yet to speak anything less is to trifle with the eternal destiny of souls. Ecumenism's promise of "unity" is tempting, but it denies Christ and paves the way for the Antichrist and his one world religion. It is a unification that will ultimately lead to destruction.

True unity is not sought by pretending that there are no differences—or any differences that are acknowledged are of no consequence—as modern ecumenists have done, but by recognizing and respecting their existence while focusing on the great orthodox truths which all Christians share. Articulated in the classic confessions and creeds, we embrace such fundamentals as the virgin birth, the deity of Christ, the atonement, the resurrection, the authority of scripture, and the second coming of Christ.

Man-made unity is not what God desires. He wants a holy people. Many Christians believe that unity in itself will bring about a holy revival, but unity cannot bring holiness. Only holiness can bring about true unity. For when God's people start seeking to live, worship and pray according to the holy Word of God, then God Himself will answer Jesus' prayer and make those who seek Him, truly "one!" THEN God will unite the hearts of those who love Him, and hate sin and error. The unification of the various national identities, races, and religions can only be achieved through the eradication of sin. That means only through the Lord Jesus Christ can we become perfectly one. The other avenue to unite people, the program of the Antichrist, will only be accomplished temporarily through spiritual deception on a towering scale.

The New Testament pattern is Gospel preaching, which includes preaching the person and work of Christ and the need to repent and believe, followed by nurturing the flock with the whole counsel of God. This is God's means of establishing true Christian unity. There will always be attacks against this unity. There were such attacks in Paul's day and Paul prophesied that such attacks would come to the Ephesians' church after his departure:

> *"Be on guard for yourselves and for all the flock, among which the Holy Spirit has made you overseers, to shepherd the church of God which He purchased with His own blood. I know that after my departure savage wolves will come in among you, not sparing the flock; and from among your own selves men will arise, speaking perverse things, to draw away the disciples after them."* *(Acts 20:28-30, NASB)*

This passage shows that first there will be attacks from within the church that will threaten Christian unity. These attacks are against the faith of the Gospel. Secondly, pastors (or elders or overseers, whatever term one uses) are commanded to guard the flock against these attacks from false teachers. The key words for church leadership, overseers, elders, and pastors, are used in Acts 20 of the same group of people.

The epistles show that Paul always publicly refuted teachings that were changes or additions to the Gospel of God's grace. God graciously saving people through the Gospel is the beginning and foundation of Christian unity. Those who teach things that are not consistent with this principle threaten true Christian unity. Paul's response to those people who preached the true Gospel with bad motives, as opposed to those who preached a false gospel, show how important it is that the Gospel is preached accurately. He rejoiced about the former (Philippians 1:18) and anathematized the latter (Galatians 1:9). The content of the Gospel is everything. If we cannot get that right, we are in grave peril! Paul writes, *"But even though we, or an angel from heaven, should preach to you a gospel contrary to that which we have preached to you, let him be accursed"* (Galatians 1:8, NASB).

In other words, Christian unity develops as sound teaching overcomes the winds of false doctrine, and Christians mature together into Christ by the speaking of truth (and, contextually, the true doctrine of God's Word) in love.

Sound doctrine gives life. False doctrine, however, is the enemy of true Christian unity, the enemy of the faith, and the enemy of our souls. Unity of faith cannot arise where false doctrine is tolerated.

A little [bad] leaven leavens the whole lump, making it unfit for consumption (e.g., Matt. 16:5–12; 1 Cor. 5.6; Gal 5:9). This is a plain reference to the power of corrupt doctrine. Likewise, water from even the purest well is rendered deadly by even a tiny amount of poison. So it is with false doctrine. *That* is why those who understand these things are 'quick to argue theology'.

*"Hold fast the pattern of sound words which you
have heard from me, in faith and love which are
in Christ Jesus. That good thing which was committed to you, keep by the Holy Spirit who dwells
in you." (2 Timothy 1:13-14, NKJV)*

The book of Revelation describes the harlot as being "drunk
with the blood of the saints" (17:6) and the blood of those who
testify of Jesus. Whether they will be martyred at the hand of
the Antichrist or by being systematically starved, believers who
are on the earth during the tribulation will experience the wrath
of the harlot and her source of power, the Antichrist. Those
who oppose the worldwide religion will be killed and those
who refuse to worship the Antichrist by accepting his mark
will be unable to buy and sell, thereby making survival very
difficult (Revelation 13:16-17).

Eventually, the harlot will lose favor with the Antichrist who
will want to receive the world's worship for himself. He will not
share the adoration of the world with the prophets and priests
of the false religion, no matter how obsequious or fawning they
may be. Once the Antichrist gains the world's amazed attention
by his miraculous return from the dead (Revelation 13:3; 12,
14), he will turn on the false religious system and destroy it,
establishing himself as God. The deception, Jesus tells us, will
be so great that, if it were possible, even the elect would fall for
it (Matthew 24:24).

Paul also taught a *separation* and *division* that few in our
day seem to know of, especially those pushing an ecumenical
unity! He taught we should *keep away from people* who cause

division and put spiritual obstacles in our way that are contrary to the apostle's doctrines:

> *"I urge you, brothers, to watch out for those who cause divisions and put obstacles in your way that are contrary to the teaching you have learned. Keep away from them. For such people are not serving our Lord Christ, but their own appetites. By smooth talk and flattery they deceive the minds of naive people." (Romans 16:17-18, NIV)*

The Apostle John, who exalted Christian love, magnified true doctrine (or teaching). Please note the spiritual harm that can be done:

> *"If anyone comes to you and does not bring this teaching, do not take him into your house or welcome him. Anyone who welcomes him shares in his wicked work." (2 John 10-11, NIV)*

Doctrine is one of the reasons why the Bible was given (2 Tim. 3:16). Moreover, the loving Lord Jesus Himself exalted true doctrine and warned against false doctrine:

> *"Be careful," Jesus said to them. "Be on your guard against the yeast of the Pharisees and Sadducees . . . . How is it you don't understand that I was not talking to you about bread? But be*

on your guard against the yeast of the Pharisees and Sadducees."... Then they understood that he was not telling them to guard against the yeast used in bread, but against the teaching of the Pharisees and Sadducees. (Matthew 16: 6, 11, 12, NIV)

While it is true that Jesus ate and drank with sinners in an effort to evangelize them, he never shared the teaching platform with false teachers or joined an organization consisting of such! Neither did any of the apostles. If the Lord Jesus or his apostles would have done so, Christians would have misunderstood such acceptance as being an endorsement of what was wrong. He then would have been lending to their credibility by not denouncing them. Christ was, and is, love incarnate, yet he is also the supreme example of uncompromising fidelity to the truth! No one publicly denounced the Pharisees like the loving Lord Jesus (Matthew. 23:1-33), who wanted unity among his true followers and prayed for such.

On the other extreme, many strict hard-line believers reject any and all platforms of ministry opportunities to bring truth into the lives of people. There are some platforms such as radio, conventions, music and televisions that have both good and false teaching and teachers. We have to be able to discern and ask God for wisdom whether to share in these venues. If we shut all the doors to reach the lost because we become so religious and judgmental in our stance where will people here the truth in a deceived world? God loves the sinner and the deceived teacher alike. His will is to save the lost (Matthew 9:13)—all of them! If we only love the righteous, what good is it?

> *"If you love those who love you, what reward will you get? Are not even the tax collectors doing that? And if you only greet your brothers, what are you doing more than others? Do not even pagans do that?" (Matthew 5:46-47, NIV)*

Life Study Lessons

1. *What is the meaning of religious unity in our secular culture?*

2. *Why can't Christianity be in unity with other religions?*

3. *Explain what Jesus meant when he said he did not come to bring peace, but a sword in Matthew 10:34:*

4. *Why can't a church be in unity with another church that teaches heresy?*

5. *Give several examples of moral or spiritual situations that caused division with others in your life:*

6. *What scriptures in the Bible tell us to stand up for sound doctrine?*

7. *Why will Christians be persecuted and killed in the end times?*

8. *What areas in your life have caused you to become a people pleaser rather than a God-pleaser?*

9. *Is it better to keep peace or make peace? What is the difference?*

10. *What spiritually happens to a person when they unite or support a false teaching or teacher?*

Chapter 5

In Counterfeit Christianity...

"Jesus said, The kingdom of heaven is likened unto a man which sowed good seed in his field: But while men slept, his enemy came and sowed tares among the wheat, and went his way. But when the blade was sprung up, and brought forth fruit, then appeared the tares also. So the servant of the household came and said unto him, Sir, didn't you sow good seed in your field? From where does it now have tares? He said to them an enemy has done this. The servants said to him, shall we go and gather them up? But he said, No; lest while you gather up the tares you up root the wheat with them. Let both grow together until the harvest: and in the time of the harvest I will say to the reapers, Gather together the tares and bind them in bundles to burn them: but gather the wheat into my barn."
(Matthew 13:24-30, NIV)

What does "counterfeit" mean? It means, made in imitation of something genuine with the intent to deceive or defraud; forged. "Counterfeit Christianity" is probably the best description we can give for a cult. Counterfeit Christianity is an imitation of real Christianity. Bible terms like "Jesus Christ", "resurrection", "salvation" and "atonement" are used by the cult, but entirely different meanings have been assigned to these terms by the various cult groups.

As counterfeit money is sometimes difficult to detect, so it is difficult to detect counterfeit Christianity, since it looks like the real thing. Experts examining counterfeit money often hold it up to a strong light and look for identifying marks. Counterfeit Christianity also has identifying marks which can be seen when held up to an even stronger light—the light of God's Word, the Bible.

How did the first forms of counterfeit Christianity emerge? "False apostles" began contradicting and undermining the teachings of the true apostles of Christ even from the very first days of the existence of the Christian church. The New Testament is filled with accounts of how false teachers and apostles arose to contend with them for the souls of the new believers. Paul cautioned the church in Rome:

> *"Now I beseech you, brethren, mark them which cause divisions and offences contrary to the doctrine which ye have learned; and avoid them. For they that are such serve not our Lord Jesus Christ, but their own belly; and by good words and fair speeches deceive the hearts of the simple. For your obedience is come abroad unto all men. I am glad therefore on your*

behalf: but yet I would have you wise unto that which is good, and simple concerning evil." (Romans 16:17-19, KJV)

The very existence of the faith and therefore the church itself was at stake. The word "heresy" literally means "division" and the church faced these counterfeits squarely and head on: Competing religious leaders, masquerading as ministers of Christ, began teaching their own false doctrines "in opposition to" Christ's apostles and His faithful servants. At first they came predominantly from a Jewish background, but then false teachers emerged from people of other backgrounds and cultures within the church. The subversive doctrines that eventually grew to be the most influential in the early church were a blend of pagan mythology and Jewish law keeping which became synthesized with the mysticism popular at that time.

Simon the Sorcerer was one such false teacher mentioned early in the scriptures. After his baptism by Philip, Simon attempted to buy the office of apostle from Peter, hoping to obtain the power to grant others the Holy Spirit. Motivated by greed for power and influence, he faked conversion and managed to receive baptism to appear Christian. In Acts 8:9-23, "But there was a certain man, called Simon, which beforetime in the same city used sorcery, and bewitched the people of Samaria, giving out that himself was some great one." Later historical sources indicate that he blended various elements of paganism and mysticism into a counterfeit Christian philosophy. A dangerous trend was established. Soon false apostles, false teachers and false brethren abounded.

A counterfeit Christianity was born and would grow at an alarming rate. In saying his farewell to the elders of the church of Ephesus, Paul stated:

> *"For I know this that after my departure savage wolves will come in among you not sparing the flock. Also from among yourselves men will rise up, speaking perverse things, to draw away the disciples after themselves. Therefore watch, and remember that for three years I did not cease to warn everyone night and day with tears". (Acts 20:29-31, KJV)*

Aaron had two sons, Nadab and Abihu. They were appointed by the priest to make fire offerings to the Lord. This was very serious business and had to be done exactly as instructed. The scripture says that they made an offering of fire unto the Lord that was not in accordance with the way it should be made. It was called "strange fire". This was a ritual they certainly knew was to be performed according to God's specific instructions but one they chose to perform in their own manner. The Bible says that this angered the Lord and that fire went out from the Him to devour them in judgment and they died before the Lord (Leviticus 10:1). Strange claims of salvation won according to human tradition, many strange varieties of personal spirituality and practice, strange and false doctrines, and strange religion are the same as "strange fire". The Lord didn't want it then and he doesn't want it now.

There are many false teachers today that are wily and

cunning counterfeit figures of "righteousness". They are a real and exceedingly dangerous reality in the church and are behind the counterfeit Christianity of today. The same kind of spiritual peril they presented to the New Testament church two millennia ago are no less deceptive, alluring, and appealing than those of today because they operate exactly the same way. They conduct themselves as paragons of virtue while cloaking sin, lust and error. Listen to the Apostle Paul's frank admonition:

> *"For such are false apostles, deceitful workers, transforming themselves into the apostles of Christ. And it is no marvel; for Satan himself is transformed into an angel of light. Therefore it is no great thing if his ministers also be transformed as the ministers of righteousness; whose end shall be according to their works" (2 Corinthians 11:13-15, KJV).*

The Apostle Peter called them "false prophets that teach damnable heresies and that many will follow their pernicious ways and with feigned words will make merchandise of you" (2 Peter 1:3, KJV). Such people today preach in our churches, operate "ministries", fill meeting places with eager disciples and, in short, look the part. And millions upon millions of Christians scarcely seem aware of this, so convinced that "we're not to judge!"

These counterfeit workers do not know or understand the gospel of grace that saves so their teaching is ultimately self-centered. They have a preoccupation with worldly concerns and advocate passionate pursuit of total self-interest. Such a carnal perspective was aptly described by the apostle John in 1 John 2:16-17:

> *"For all that is in the world, the lust of the flesh, and the lust of the eyes, and the pride of life, is not of the Father, but is of the world. And the world passeth away, and the lust thereof: but he that doeth the will of God abideth for ever."* *(KJV)*

Ninety percent of the teaching in churches today is about the "Christian life" and how to live it, but it usually revolves around how to pursue some manner of lifestyle based upon a view of a sugar-daddy God whose hands-off approach to our lives perfectly represents the kind of God whom self-centered Christians want Him to be. This is satanic because it turns people's eyes onto themselves in the worst possible way. We are all helpless sinners and there is no way to derive true spiritual aid through our own power or our own wisdom. The work of the Spirit is to point us to Christ and to glorify Him. The Spirit does not speak of Himself, nor will one who is filled by His Spirit (John 16:13). Satan wants you to be ineffective, and ineffective is what you will be if you look to yourself for strength, direction or salvation. Christ is our only strength and our only hope.

The Gospel is about Jesus Christ, His life, His death, His resurrection, and His position at the right hand of God. The Gospel calls into question all that we think and do as Christians.

It is the deciding factor as to who is a real Christian and who is a counterfeit. There is only one Gospel and there is only one way to believe and have faith. The Apostle Paul said, *"But even if we, or an angel from heaven, preach any other gospel to you than what we have preached to you, let him be accursed"* (Galatians 1:6-9, NKJV). There is no room for any kind of strange fire here. We must know beyond a shadow of a doubt how, and what, the Lord wants us to believe and exercise faith in it—for upon this our very souls depend.

Counterfeit Spirituality

Many New Age teachings are entering Christian churches in North America by introducing occult concepts through innocent-appearing, refreshing new innovations. One of these uses the notion of "prayer walks" confined to what are called labyrinths. Labyrinths are walkways combining spirals and circles in a maze like pattern that are used as places for Christians to practice self-introspective meditation as they walk through it. Those that teach their use offer them as "another type of prayer", or as "prayer in motion." Most think of a labyrinth as a maze-like area with winding paths and dead ends where the journey itself becomes the destination, compelling personal transformation and spiritual growth by going deep into personal self-exploration. Non-Christian practitioners of the prayer labyrinth, also known as a meditation labyrinth, use them regularly as mystical ritual and spiritual growth based upon self-introspection and self-centering meditation. This is a longstanding reality within many occult circles globally.

At its core, a labyrinth walk is not aimed at orthodox Christian prayer to the God of the Bible while walking down the sidewalk. The symbolism has been used to infect spiritual aspirants of Christian persuasion with the notion that it is essentially, in some way, an affirmation of God's presence. It was never understood to teach such a thing, however, and to New Age disciples a labyrinth represents the "path of life." As one travels the labyrinth's "path of life", it leads their walk to the center of an intricate design representing the center of one's innermost self then exiting back along the same path. A prayer or meditation Labyrinth only has one route or single path. Again, unlike the maze, a Labyrinth is designed with one destination and is impossible to get lost within. It doesn't need any concept of deity whatsoever to be used and is enthusiastically observed by people seeking enlightenment without any acknowledgment of the Lordship of Jesus Christ. It is a form of self-centering spirituality that rejects any connection with the Biblical perspective on the fallen nature of man.

Openness to spiritual phenomenon that provides vital connection to the spiritual world is another major concept sweeping our land. From fascination with angels to contact with the dead, the never ending clamour of Christians seeking after spiritual experiences has long been a fruitful source for false teachers, whose stirring tales of extra-Biblical visitations and spiritual power also boldly claim this is "scriptural" through one of many scriptures such as:

*"Most assuredly, I say to you, hereafter you shall
see heaven open, and the angels of God ascending*

and descending upon the Son of Man." (John 1:51, NKJV)

"After these things I looked, and behold, a door standing open in heaven. And the first voice which I heard was like a trumpet speaking with me, saying "Come up here, and I will show you things which must take place after this. Immediately, I was in the spirit." (Revelation 4:1-2, NKJV)

They teach that the "door" in the book of Revelation suggests God's invitation for us to have access to His heavenly realm. Also, as His friends, the Lord supposedly wants to open the portals of Heaven and release an unparalleled visitation of heavenly hosts. These un-Biblical claims using scripture, twisted out of context, have become a major source of deception in the church today and have plagued it with an entire sub-culture of misguided church movements led by misguided church leaders. Worst of all this arousal of an illegitimate fascination with the spiritual world and the beings dwelling within them has actually helped foster an entry into the demonic. Unfortunately, this type of teaching is being endorsed by major Christian media across the globe.

The Gospel is a very simple message. Christ has saved us by doing for us that which we are not capable of doing for ourselves, because we were dead in trespasses and sins (Ephesians 2:1). By His righteous life He has offered everything to the Godhead that the law required in our name and on our behalf.

Jesus, the Christ, is the "new Adam" and the only perfect representative of the human race (Romans 5:12-21), whose death on the cross was as our great substitute. Since the failure of the "old Adam", our fallen race utterly failed to measure up to God's law—but His love found a way to deliver us through the blood of Jesus. We are saved by His sacrifice on the cross and not by anything we can do ourselves. By His crucifixion, He took our old sinful, Adamic nature and put it to death. Our old life of failure is buried in Joseph's new tomb. When Christ died we, by faith, we died with Him. The apostle Paul said, "I am been crucified with Christ: nevertheless I live..." (Galatians 2:20, KJV). The sin problem has been dealt with and Satan has been defeated (Romans 6:1-7). When Christ came out of the tomb we came out with Him (Romans 6:5). This is not rocket science but the simple message of the Gospel. This is what the Lord wants you to believe and have faith in.

What about my Christian life, some ask? Colossians 3:1 exhorts that if you have risen with Christ, you should seek those things which are above, where Christ sits at the right hand of God. Verses 3 through 4 conclude, therefore, that if you are dead in Christ that your life is hid with Christ, in God. It beautifully states that "when Christ who is our life, shall appear, then shall you also appear with Him in glory." This is where your Christian life is—or should be. It is, or can be, in a very safe and secure place.

If your life truly is in heaven with Christ you should act like it. Why? Because we are complete in Him and in Him alone. Play your position (Colossians 2:10)! Too much is made out of what we "do" in the Christian life, as if there was some kind of greatness within ourselves. We have nothing to glory in and we have nothing to offer the Lord apart from what His grace gives us. If the Apostle Paul, who was the world's greatest Christian, referred to himself as a wretched sinner, where does that leave you and me? Christ has done it all. Knowing this, how should we now live? The Apostle Paul said, "The life which I now live in the flesh I live by faith in the son of God who loved me and gave himself for me." The Christian life is a life of rest, a rest in what Christ has accomplished for us as in Hebrews 4:5-11.

So the world and the apostate church's rejection of these essential Christian tenets and others, such as the historical definition of God as Triune, should be a major warning sign to any perceptive believer. Another sobering sign, hidden in plain sight, is the existence of thousands of cultic groups that deny the Christian Gospel to pursue their own warped interpretations. These deceptive sects may vary in size from a handful of people meeting in a private home to massive international movements, but all of them share in the denial of the deity of Christ, and of the Trinity, and they all typi- cally follow in point-by-point succession each of the other characteristics we'll discuss now in this chapter.

The Apostle Paul said, "That if we or an angel from heaven preach any other gospel let him be accursed" in Galatians 1:6-9. There is no room for any kind of strange fire here. We must know beyond a shadow of a doubt how and what the Lord wants us to believe, because our very souls depend upon this.

The rejection of fundamental Christian tenets such as the classical definition of God should be a major warning sign to any perceptive believer. Groups that deny the Christian viewpoint of the deity of Christ and the Trinity typically follow in point-by-point succession with each of the other characteristics in this article. One example is The Way International, a group founded by Victor Paul Wierwille, (who once served as a former evangelical pastor). In fact, several cult leaders had their start in authentic Christian denominations and churches. Wierwille denies that there are three persons in the Godhead. He also claimed that Jesus was not God, teaching that the deity of Christ was not a Christian teaching for the Christian church's first 300 years. This is a common (though false) assertion of many cult leaders. Because Wierwille and his church deny the very essence of what makes God who He is, this is a group to avoid.

Although a counterfeit doctrine may include the idea that God's grace is important in the role of salvation, the leader normally emphasizes the idea that "salvation" ultimately comes through one's own efforts. Take, for instances, devotees of Hare Krishna. These dedicated followers believe that they are in the middle stage of their reincarnation cycle. The way for a dedicated devotee to be born into the next level of existence is to deny himself on this earth while performing good works, including the repetition of the Hare Krishna mantra a total of 1,728 times a day. It may take a devotee who wakes up at 4 A.M. several hours a day to maintain this goal. Those who belong to such work-oriented groups are normally told that they can never know if their works are good enough to please God; instead, they are told to keep trying even harder.

Counterfeit Christian churches often make it a point to cast doubt and suspicion on other churches or denominations, with the leader oftentimes claiming that only his church is true. While many groups hold that the Christian churches do have partial truth, it is taught that full truth has somehow been lost and can now only be found in the "one true church" or the "restoration". This may involve utilizing Christian terminology while having a different meaning behind those particular words. A prime example of this is the Watchtower Society, also known as the Jehovah's Witnesses. This group, founded by Charles Taze Russell in the 19th-century, teaches that those who belong to any church outside of "Jehovah's" church are doomed to annihilation. Only those who belong to the Watchtower organization have a chance to attain "Paradise Earth." This is why Jehovah's Witnesses are adamant in sharing their faith door to door, even attempting to convert those who already attend Christian churches. The Jehovah's Witnesses will often use words that sound reasonable to a nominal Christian (i.e. "Jehovah's Christian Witnesses," "salvation," "Jesus Christ," etc), but they are usually reluctant to tell potential converts that the meanings behind these words are completely different than what has been historically meant.

A group where the leader(s) has an authoritative role, even to the extent that they say they speak for God, is another cause for concern. Such leaders claim to have "special revelations" with God, and their words hold special precedence over their followers. A classic example is Jim Jones, who led almost 1,000 followers to their deaths in the jungle of Guyana in 1978. When men in his charge killed Rep. Leo Ryan (D-CA), a congressman who was visiting "Jonestown" in response to complaints from the relatives of church members, Jones called for his followers to drink cyanide-laced Kool-Aid. The majority of the people willingly followed his commands because they had come to accept his words as truthful and from God. Those who refused were shot. Trusting someone to the degree that you listen to any command—even to the point of moving to another country and then taking your own life—is something which God never intended.

Another heretical trait is when a church regulates the giving of its people or requires a certain amount of financial giving in order to receive certain privileges related to salvation or "enlightenment". For example, the Church of Scientology teaches that people need to discover their true nature through a process called "auditing". This is accomplished by "clearing Engrams" from one's life. One *Los Angeles Times* article on Scientology estimated that it would cost a full "Operating Thetan 8" participant $200,000 to $400,000 from the beginning of the lessons through their completion. Without these courses, the adherent is unable to clear himself of these unwanted "Engrams." Using finances as a requirement to reach salvation goals is completely opposed to what Jesus, Paul, and Peter preached.

Many counterfeit Christian churches insist that if a member decides to leave the group, for whatever reason, they jeopardize their salvation before God. An example of this damaging and presumptuous doctrine is found in the culture the Church of Jesus Christ of Latter-day Saints (The Mormons). As long as a person continues to remain Mormon and works hard to attain salvation, including the performance of work at one of the temples, salvation is just around the corner. But if a person leaves the church, he not only could lose his family relationships, including marriage, children, friends, etc, but the celestial kingdom. They also teach the very best a person can desire, is also lost. In fact, while it is believed that most people will not be sent to "Outer Darkness," which is a hell-like eternal state mainly reserved for Satan and his followers. Early Mormon leaders claimed that this was a place apostates could go, especially if they said bad things about the Mormon Church. Holding a person's salvation hostage in such a way is certainly not Biblical.

Although the Bible is frequently utilized and even considered beneficial by a number of counterfeit groups, it is not considered completely authoritative. Therefore, extra-biblical writings are necessary. Normally these scriptures are considered to have more authority than the dated Bible. The Christian Science religion is one example. Those who inquire into this religion are told that Mary Baker Eddy's 1875 pantheistic book *Science and Health with Key to the Scriptures* is a *"reference book for life,"* which is needed by a person who hopes to discover *"practical, spiritual answers for health and healing, security, and lasting relationships."* This book must be studied in order to ascertain full truth. When the Bible contradicts Eddy's book, then the Bible is considered to be wrong or misunderstood.

The idea that a "hidden mystery" or "new truth" is available through a particular church should be taken as a strong sign that this group is a counterfeit Christian religion. In addition, many such groups may change their doctrines over time. Christians believe that God has very clearly shown His truth through the pages of the Bible; therefore, new or fluctuating doctrine—especially that which contradicts the Bible—ought to be taken with a great deal of caution. The Unification Church (numerous front names include "Association of Families for Unification and World Peace" or "Family Federation for World Peace and Unification") was founded by Korean, "Rev." Sun Myung Moon. He taught that Jesus never fulfilled his mission. Therefore, Moon said that he was commissioned to finish the job that Jesus never finished. Moon's followers (often known as "Moonies") accepted Moon as a Christ-like representative on earth whose teachings supersede the Bible. This apostate "church" actively recruits through a wide variety of front groups using impressive names such as the "Association of Families for Unification and World Peace" or "Family Federation for World Peace and Unification". The Unification Church theology has evolved over time. This phenomenon is also infiltrating the Christian church globally. You will especially find this "new revelation" teaching in the latter rain revival movement, the apostolic and prophetic movement and the dominion theology movement.

Dominion Theology

They believe the Gospel of Salvation is achieved by setting up the "Kingdom of God" as a *literal and physical kingdom* to be "advanced" on Earth in the present age. Some dominionists liken the New Testament Kingdom to the Old Testament Israel in ways that justify taking up the sword, or other methods of punitive judgment, to war against enemies of their kingdom. Dominionists teach that men can be coerced or compelled to enter the kingdom. They assign to the church duties and rights that belong scripturally only to Jesus Christ. This includes the esoteric belief that believers can "incarnate" Christ and function as His body on earth to establish His kingdom rule. An inordinate emphasis is placed on man's efforts; the doctrine of the sovereignty of God is diminished.

Dominion theology is predicated upon three basic beliefs: 1) Satan usurped man's dominion over the earth through the temptation of Adam and Eve; 2) The church is God's instrument to take dominion back from Satan; 3) Jesus cannot or will not return until *the church* has taken dominion by *gaining control of the earth's governmental and social institutions*. [emphasis added]

Al Dager, *Vengeance Is Ours: The Church in Dominion*

Dominion theology is a *heresy*. As such it is rarely presented as openly as the definitions above may indicate. Outside of the reconstructionist camp, evangelical dominionism has wrapped itself in slick packages—one piece at a time—for mass-media consumption. This has been a slow process, taking several decades. Few evangelicals would recognize the word "dominionism" or know what it means. This is because other terminologies have been developed which soft-sell dominionism, concealing the full scope of the agenda. Many evangelicals (and even their more conservative counterparts, the fundamentalists) may adhere to tidbits of dominionism without recognizing the error. This is because dominionism has "crept in unawares" (Jude 4) to seduce an undiscerning generation.

Spiritual Warfare Movement

The "Kingdom of God" must be advanced on earth through hyper-spiritual "warfare" activities against the devil. A veritable supermarket of verbal and physical prayer techniques such as chanting, walks, and marches are employed in this effort. Believers are told their prayer power creates spiritual "canopies" over regions, preparing the way for "revival." In this sense, prayer warfare is seen as preparatory work so that the other two movements can build the kingdom. Recently the contemplative prayer movement–which includes meditation, fasting, and labyrinths–has been brought into the spiritual warfare prayer "arsenal." Prayer serves as a convenient decoy for covert operations.

Promoting these prayer warfare activities are hyper-charismatic's from the "signs and wonders" movement, which include self-anointed, self-appointed "apostles" and "prophets" who are preparing to govern the world through their "New Apostolic Reformation." This dominionist sect is a direct offshoot of the Latter Rain cult (also known as Joel's Army or Manifest Sons of God).

The Manifest Sons of God of the Latter Rain Movement

Here is the underlying goal within the Latter Rain message of Bill Hamon:

> *"The whole creation is waiting for the last generation church. The earth and all of creation*

are waiting for **the manifestation of God's last-day apostles and prophets** *and <u>fully restored church</u>. "For the earnest expectation of the creation eagerly waits for the revealing of the sons of God" (Romans 8:19 NKJV). When the Church is fully restored, <u>then the saints will receive their final redemption, the immortalization of their mortal bodies</u>. When this happens, then the natural creation of plants and animals will be delivered from their bondage of corruption into the glorious liberty of the children of God." (Hamon, Bill. Apostles, Prophets and the Coming Moves of God: God's End-Time Plans for His Church and Planet Earth. Destiny Image Publishers, 1997, p. 235)*

"The Earth and all of creation is waiting for the manifestation of the sons of God, the time when they will come into their maturity and immortalization... When the church receives its full inheritance and redemption then creation will be redeemed from its cursed condition of decay, change and death... the church has a responsibility and ministry to the rest of creation. Earth and its natural creation is anxiously waiting for the church to reach full maturity and come to full son-ship. **When the church realizes its full son-ship, its bodily redemption will cause a redemptive chain reaction throughout all of**

creation." (Hamon, Bill. *The Eternal Church:*
Destiny Image Publishers, 2011, p. 385)

How do we reach this maturity? They say by the apostles
and prophets. Seems to be circular reasoning. To a certain
extent this is true of what will happen, but what Hamon says
when and how it will happen is not true.

Hamon promotes one of the more distorted doctrines that
came from the Latter Rain movement, the *Manifested Sons of
God* doctrine. Their interpretation of this verse is unique in
church history. There is no rapture but people will be changed
into eternal beings right here on earth to do miraculous works
like Jesus to overcome the devil and the world system BEFORE
the Lord returns.

In his book, *The Eternal Church*, Hamon claims "Jesus is
waiting on the church. All that the fall of man and sin has taken
away from humanity, Jesus, through His church shall restore."

Again this can only take place "**When the church realizes
its full son-ship, its bodily redemption will cause a redemptive chain reaction throughout all of creation**." (p. 385)

Their belief is that a certain group of Christians will obtain
immortality by incarnating Christ before He returns. How?
Obedience to the Apostles and Prophets. What is it that all
creation is waiting for? According to orthodox Christianity
all creation awaits the removal of the "Curse of futility", sin
placed upon it by God from the Fall of Adam. What they
neglect in this verse is the context along with support from the
other passages of this event. *"Not only that, but we also who
have the firstfruits of the Spirit, even we ourselves groan within*

ourselves, *eagerly waiting for the adoption, the redemption of our body*." (Romans 8:23, NKJV)

Concerning the adoption of the redeeming of our body, here are a few examples of the truth in God's Word:

How will it happen? 1 Cor.15:51-54; 1 Thess. 4:16-17: *"For the Lord Himself will descend from heaven with a shout, with the voice of an archangel, and with the trumpet of God. And the dead in Christ will rise first. Then we who are alive and remain shall be caught up together with them in the clouds to meet the Lord in the air. And thus we shall always be with the Lord."* (NKJV)

When will it happen? Phil. 3:20-21: *"For our citizenship is in heaven, from which we also eagerly wait for the Savior, the Lord Jesus Christ, who will transform our lowly body that it may be conformed to His glorious body, according to the working by which He is able even to subdue all things to Himself."* (NKJV)

Heb.9:28: *"so Christ was offered once to bear the sins of many. To those who eagerly wait for Him He will appear a second time, apart from sin, for salvation."* (NKJV) It is Christ who appears and changes us, not some event separate from this. We wait for Him; we cannot accomplish this on our own!!!

It's not the church that does this but Jesus himself. And it will not be complete until all who are in Christ are resurrected.

Hamon states:

> "At that time the sons of God will be fully mani-
> fested on the earth. *Widespread spiritual warfare
> will result with the sons of God doing battle with*

Satan and company, the non-Christian nations of this world will also be defeated. <u>Once the earth has been subdued, Jesus will come back to earth and be given the kingdom that has been won for Him by this "manchild company</u>." The Manifested Sons of God doctrine teaches that these sons will be equal to Jesus Christ: immortal, sinless, perfected sons who have partaken of the divine nature. <u>They will have every right to be called **gods and will be called gods**</u>." (Prophets and the Prophetic Movement Bill Hamon).

Is that how the Scripture explains it—or does Jesus come back, Satan is vanquished, the kingdom commences because he rids evil on the earth (Matthew 25,) and only those saved go into the millennium and he rules over all the earth?

You thought that there was only one God—but in the latter rain movement every initiate becomes a Jesus (a manifestation of the sons of God. Romans 8:19). And who is calling them gods? The Bible never calls creatures gods. Who wants us to think we will be gods? Could it be the one who brought the first sin into the world?

Paul Cain who worked with Branham brought this same teaching into the Vineyard churches "I want you to know <u>He's coming to the church before He comes FOR the church</u>. He's gonna perfect the church so the church can be the Image, <u>and be Him</u>, and be his representation." (Cain, Paul: *My Father's House*, 1988. Tape.)

Joel's Army

Remember the song that went, "Oh when the saints, come marchin' in, oh when the saints come marchin in, Lord I want to be in that number when the saints come marchin' in." This is not the tune you'll find Joel's army sings because they are not looking to be brought up to Jesus but waiting for Christ (the anointing) to be brought down upon them to march through the land.

The church that once looked toward being taken away to heaven (John14) has been taught by some to change her focus. In about the mid-70's, a triumphant post-millennial doctrine appeared. Instead of watching for the blessed coming of the Lord the goal became to establish the kingdom on earth. Doctrines about the rapture, tribulation, an end time apostasy with a literal personal antichrist were taught as deceptions. Without a tribulation ahead, there is no need to be vigilant, discerning or watchful. With no apostasy, there is no need to look for deception, only blessing. The desire for heavenly things has faded out, and "Restorationist" Christians no longer "look up". They look around them and consider how to transform the world and rule over it. When Christ comes back they will hand over a Christian earth.

Not all Dominionists, Charismatics and Restorationists believe the same things, especially how it is to be accomplished. Few still believe in the rapture, but there are many variables. So I'm not addressing all, but a certain group that has mainly been affiliated with the Vineyard, the prophetic/apostolic movement from Kansas City and the Latter Rain teachers.

The "Latter Rain" movement is run on the rail of misinterpreted Scriptures and spiritualizing their context. Hosea 6:3 tells us the Lord will come as the latter rain, and James 5:7 speaks of the Latter Rain, but ties it together with the coming of the Lord. The "former and latter rain" refers to the agricultural calendar of the land of Israel although it has a spiritual truth. The latter rain was essential for bountiful crop harvest in Israel. This corresponds to the giving of the Spirit at Pentecost as Peter proclaimed this is like that of Joel but was not the ultimate fulfillment. Joel 2:23 also speaks of a harvest of abundance, but the modern interpreters have given Joel's army new significance. Joel's army will purge the earth (the cleansing) of all wickedness and rebellion and even judge the apostate church (which is those who do not join their fraternity of miracle workers). They will overcome death itself, they will redeem all creation, and restore the earth. The church will inherit the earth, and rule the nations all before Christ comes back. When He (Jesus) does come we are to hand the kingdom over to Him and He will say, "job well done, enter into the kingdom". The real Joel's army in Joel 2 does NO miracles and marches strictly through the land of Israel making destruction; there is no blessing from Joel's army marching. If one reads through about Joel's army they find that they will be destroyed in the end.

Because Joel's army is called God's army they think that they are His people. In the same way Cyrus was called God's shepherd (Isa.44:28, he was given all the kingdoms of the earth (Ezra 1:2, 2 Chron.36:23). He was called Gods anointed (Isa. 45:1*); "Thus says the LORD to <u>His anointed, to Cyrus, whose</u>*

right hand I have held—to subdue nations before him and loose the armor of kings, to open before him the double doors, so that the gates will not be shut." Sounds familiar? Nebuchadnezzar was also called God's servant (Jer. 43:10), *"and say to them, 'Thus says the LORD of hosts, the God of Israel: "Behold, I will send and bring Nebuchadnezzar the king of Babylon, My servant, and will set his throne above these stones that I have hidden. And he will spread his royal pavilion over them"* (NASB). One must consider the actions of these men's teachings in light of what Joel is actually saying. So despite their new interpretation, the Bible's definition still stands. They may be called God's army but they are not his people. Joel's army is the raising up of a devouring army of locusts, (destroyers) to bring judgment upon the land. Whether Israel or the church, it's not good.

Much of this is being preached from the pulpits, big and small, without the congregant's ever blinking. Without being able to identify phrases they don't know what they are ingesting. Many churches have turned into "Latter Rain" churches by default or influence—some knowingly and some not.

"In the near future we will not be looking back at the early church with envy because of the great exploits of those days, but all will be saying that He certainly did save the best wine for last. The most glorious times in all of history have not come upon us. You, who have dreamed of one day being able to talk with Peter, John and Paul, are going to be surprised to find that they have

all been waiting to talk to you." (Joyner, Rick, The Harvest Morning Star, 1990)

This means the apostles were not special in starting the church and having divine miracles...we are. Think about the ramifications of this proposal. This means if the church began with them and today's church with its SUPER apostles and prophets will do greater things. Then the church really begins all over again.

Nowhere does scripture teach that the church will do wonders like this in the end. Jesus actually WARNED that these signs and wonders at the end are to DECEIVE THE ELECT (Matthew24). Is anyone paying attention to the scriptures and the times we are living in?

Mormons are not the only ones who have false modern apostles. John, a true apostle, said the church did. Rev.2:2 *"And you have tested those who say they are apostles and are not, and have found them liars;"* (NKJV) Notice John says they have tested them. Paul said the church did as well 2 Cor. 11:13 *"For such are false apostles, deceitful workers, transforming themselves into apostles of Christ."* (NKJV) Notice Paul says they transform themselves to look like they do. How? By their teaching, authority and could very well have had manifestations of power.

" The early church was a firstfruits offering, truly this will be a harvest! It was said of the Apostle Paul that he was turning the world upside down; <u>it will be said of the apostles soon to be anointed</u>

*that they have turned an upside down world right
side up." (Rick Joyner, The Harvest, 128-129)*

So from what I can gather Joyner says that they are going to reverse what the Apostle Paul did.

What if it's me or you?

What is most tragic is the fact that the majority of those who see themselves as "born again believers" are, in fact, part of the apostate church. The words "born again" and "Christian" flow so easily from the lips of church people today, but many have been deceived. They have accepted as "truth" a multitude of false doctrines without questioning the messages they hear. It is too easy to accept the messages of the "anointed" ministers that are so quick to say, "Thus saith the Lord." Jesus told of those very "ministers" when He said that "many in that day" would say to Him, "Lord, Lord, we did all these things in your Name." But Jesus' reply to them will be, "Depart from me. I never knew you."

In the world of the Cults, there are two classes of people. At the high levels, we find the *DECEIVERS*. At the lower levels, we find the DECEIVED. Remember, you will usually be dealing with the honest-hearted DECEIVED ones, so remember our instructions in 2 Timothy 2: 24-26:

*"And the Lord's bond-servant must not be quar-
relsome, but be kind to all, able to teach, patient
when wronged, with gentleness correcting those*

who are in opposition, if perhaps God may grant them repentance, leading to the knowledge of the truth, and they may come to their senses and escape from the snare of the devil, having been held captive by him to do his will." (NASB)

Not all counterfeits may be characterized by every one of these traits. However, a person should be cautious when considering a church that is marked by one or two of these characteristics, especially any of the first three in the list above. Churches with three or more of the above characteristics ought to be avoided at all cost.

In addition, there are some Christian churches that may not have doctrinal problems but are rather sociological abusers. For instance, some churches have controlling "discipleship" programs or church memberships with high levels of guilt or feelings of inadequacy. These types of groups also ought to be avoided. If you believe that your church has problems in either doctrinal or sociological areas, you would be wise not to get involved. If you are already a member, you need to consider leaving. As John 8:31-32 says, *"Then said Jesus to those Jews which believed on him, If ye continue in my word, then are ye my disciples indeed; And ye shall know the truth, and the truth shall make you free." (KJV)*

Remember that persons who have been led into cults have gone because they were sincerely seeking for God, and no true Christian bore witness to them. Or, after receiving Christ they received wrong teaching, supposing that what they did pleased God. Cults are clever counterfeits for those not grounded solidly in Biblical teachings. It is not too late to lead them to the true Christ, or win them back to their original commitment. Where there is life, there is always hope.

Sound Doctrine

Satan hates God's law. He is a master deceiver from the beginning in the Garden of Eden. Naturally, he will spare no effort to infiltrate the churches that Jesus Christ has established.

To accomplish his purpose, Satan uses people to mislead other people. It is easy for him to influence human beings who desire to teach others when they are motivated by personal ambition rather than a pure heart and the "great commission" that Jesus commanded for His disciples. This is true if they lack proper understanding of the scriptures. The enemy takes advantage of them because they desire to be spiritual teachers. He seduces susceptible individuals to pay lip service to Christ while they create their own new sets of beliefs and doctrines while ignoring or disobeying portions of the scriptures or God's law.

Paul told Timothy to "charge some that they teach no other doctrine" and have a "pure heart", "good conscience", and "sincere faith...from which some having strayed, have turned aside to idle talk, desiring to be teachers of the law, understanding neither what they say nor the things which they affirm." (1 Timothy 1:3, 6, 7, NKJV)

Sincere but misguided religious leaders can and do create doctrinal error which, in their minds, permit them to break some of God's commandments. Once they are in this deception they persuade others to do the same. Through the devil's influence, they persuade themselves and others that their concepts and beliefs are righteous. They believe that God is pleased with them while they believe the false doctrines they teach. Some of these teachers are sincere—but they are sincerely wrong.

Paul says:

> *"The coming of the lawless one is according to the working of Satan, with all power, signs, and lying wonders, and with all unrighteous deception among those who perish, because they did not receive the love of the truth, that they might be saved. And for this reason God will send them strong delusion, that they should believe the lie..." (2 Thessalonians 2:9-11, NKJV)*

By creating a counterfeit religion, especially one that is not entirely different from the true church but rejects some of the essential Biblical teachings that lead to eternal life, Satan is attempting to corrupt and thwart God's plan for eternal life for the souls of men. *"And he said unto him, Why callest thou me good? there is none good but one, that is, God: but if thou wilt enter into life, keep the commandments."* (Matthew 19:17, KJV). This is what the enemy wants to create. He promotes lawless Christianity that teaches that we can selectively obey or even ignore God's commandments in the scriptures. Satan's purpose is to convince people that they are serving Christ and cutting off true salvation from them by clouding their understanding of what sin is so they will continue to be in sin. These people will continue to practice at least some degree of lawlessness.

Satan retains just enough truth to persuade or convince someone they are following Christ but he introduces enough deception to keep them to meet the conditions of obeying God's Word that He requires as a condition to inherit eternal life.

Remember to fight SPIRITUAL BATTLES with SPIRITUAL WEAPONS. Prayer is your chief weapon. Take your authority as a Christian and bind the spirit of deception operating in the cultist's life, loosing him/her to hear the Gospel of Christ (See Matthew 18:18-20). Prepare yourself to witness as the Holy Spirit makes opportunity for you, by becoming acquainted with cult views on Christ and salvation, as well as the scriptures to correct these views.

One of the ministries of the Holy Spirit is to CONVICT the world of SIN. If the reading of the above causes some pain in your heart of hearts, take it as a wake-up call, from the love of the Most High God, calling you to back away from the edge of the dark abyss. If anything (or many things) in the above passages causes an internal twinge, a feeling of guilt, know that it is not condemnation; it is conviction... think of it as a heavenly laser beam that just pierced through a hard covering over an area within you, where un-confessed sins have been hidden—sins that you have not faced, acknowledged, confessed and repented of. Beloved, these need to be dealt with! This is the part that you must do!

The Counterfeit Modern Gospel doesn't tell you of the need for you to do your part (i.e., acknowledging, confessing, and repenting of all <u>your</u> particular past and present sins), before Jesus Christ can do His part, which is forgiveness, and cleansing in that area. Failure to do your part, to confess your disobedience (sin) in any area of your mind, any area of your heart, any area of your soul, any area of your spirit, any area of your body, leaves you wide open for the curses of disobedience to influence your body and rage in your life, effecting not only your own circumstances, but those for whom you are responsible. People assume that all, or at least almost all, who bear the name Christian follow the beliefs, teachings and practices of Jesus Christ. The Bible, however, tells us that not everyone who accepts the name of Christ is really a Christian!

Jesus foretold that some would claim His name but deny Him by their actions. He said they would "call Me 'Lord, Lord,' but "not do the things which I say" (Luke 6:46). Christ and His apostles spoke of *false prophets, false apostles* and *false brethren.* They revealed that two opposing religions would emerge, both claiming to be Christian. One—the actual church Jesus founded—would be led by God's Spirit and remain faithful to His teachings. The other—guided and influenced by a different spirit—would accept the *name* of Christ but twist His teachings to create a convincing *counterfeit* of the true church of God.

> *"For if someone comes to you and preaches a Jesus other than the Jesus we preached, or if you receive a different spirit from the one you received, or a different gospel from the one you accepted, you put up with it easily enough."*
> *(2 Corinthians 11:4, NIV)*

In this verse Paul is saying…the false teachers do not even pretend they have "another Jesus" and a "different Gospel" to bring before you; they merely try to supplant me, your accredited Teacher. Yet ye not only "bear with" them, but **prefer** them instead of exposing their false teaching or marking them as false teachers. They prefer false teachers over the "Truth".

Both would use Christ's name and claim His authority. Both would perform works that would outwardly appear good and right. Both would claim to be following Christ's true teachings. But only one would faithfully represent its founder, Jesus Christ. The other would capture the minds and hearts of humanity by attaching the name of Christ to Biblically insupportable religious customs and doctrines that Jesus and His apostles neither practiced nor approved. If your desire is to become a follower of the true Gospel, you must acknowledge that you've missed the narrow way; you must allow the Holy Spirit to take you back to the drawing board, with thanksgiving for being awakened to your error. There is still an opportunity to "redeem the time" that has been lost. May the Comforter, the Counselor, the Spirit of Truth continue to reveal all that you have missed by following the "Counterfeit Modern Gospel." May the Wisdom of God empower you to be obedient to what you find, in a deliberate and timely manner, without distractions and side trips that you may precede to the next rung on the ladder, with renewed purpose, resolve and focus.

Testing the spirits

Testing doctrine is very important to every person who is interested in living by the truth of God. Truth must be known in order to be lived (John 8:31-32). But, to know truth we must be willing to test what is offered to us as truth in order to determine if it is, in fact, the truth of God.

The Bible teaches us to prove all things so that we may hold fast to what is good and abstain from every form of evil (1 Thessalonians 5:21-22). We should pray to abound in knowledge and discernment so that we can distinguish between what is right and what is wrong (Philippians 1:9-10). "Beloved, believe not every spirit, but try the spirits whether they are of God: because many false prophets are gone out into the world" (1 John 4:1). Every preacher or teacher should be willing to have his teaching examined for its accuracy (1 Timothy 4:16). Unfortunately, such is not always the case.

Many people who want to live in the truth have not properly tested the doctrine they accept. Some of them test doctrine to see whether it is true by how it makes them feel (Proverbs 14:12). Others use tradition to determine right and wrong (Matthew 15:1-3). Still others determine the validity of doctrine on the basis of human wisdom and philosophy (1 Corinthians 1:21; Colossians 2:8). Some base truth upon whether the doctrine in question is popular (Galatians 1:10). Some expect to receive a "prompting in the heart" telling them whether something is truth or error. Their eyes have been blinded so that they cannot see the light of the Gospel (2 Corinthians 4:3-4). In contrast, here are biblical ways to test the accuracy of doctrine:

Does it agree with what the apostolic doctrine of the first century found in the New Testament?

"We are of God: he that knows God hears us; he who is not of God hears us not. BY THIS WE KNOW the spirit of truth, and the spirit of error" (1 John 4:6). It was the "apostles' doctrine" in which the early Christians "continued steadfastly" (Acts 2:42). They had been taught it, they had knowledge of it, and so they could live it and use it to test what others taught them. We must learn and know the apostles' doctrine - it is our God-given instrument of testing to avoid being tossed about and destroyed by error (Ephesians 4:14).

We now have the apostles' doctrine in the form of inspired scripture (1 Corinthians 14:37).

The scriptures must be used to establish doctrine and to equip us to do every good work (2 Timothy 3:16-17). When we use the scriptures to test doctrine we are using an objective standard. It is the same truth for everybody. Compare this with the false ways of testing doctrine mentioned above (feelings, tradition, human wisdom, popularity, and "promptings" of the heart). There is a big difference between doctrine that changes depending on who is talking and doctrine which remains the same for everyone! (1 Peter 1:22-25)

Jesus warned us against false prophets in Matthew 7:15-23. Please read this passage carefully. The standard we must use when testing prophets (teachers, preachers, etc.) is the will of the Father - the Gospel (v. 21). It is the standard that measures every man. Everyone who does not conform to it will be rejected by Jesus (v. 23). The "fruit" the prophet bears must harmonize with the Father's will, the Gospel (v. 16-20).

Don't accept man's word as truth - test it with God's Word! (Galatians 1:6-10)

> *"By their fruit you will recognize them. Do people pick grapes from thorn bushes, or figs from thistles? Likewise every good tree bears good fruit, but a bad tree bears bad fruit. A good tree cannot bear bad fruit, and a bad tree cannot bear good fruit. Every tree that does not bear good fruit is cut down and thrown into the fire. Thus, by their fruit you will recognize them."*
> *(Matthew 7:16-20, NIV)*

Test the lives of those pretending to be sent by God. Are there inconsistencies in their lives? Are their lives in agreement with God's Word? Are they receiving glory for what they do, or is God receiving glory? Are they relying on God only for direction or are they basing their teachings on writings from men? Are they or their followers putting their word above the Bible? The Spirit of God always speaks in accordance to God's Word, the Bible. He acknowledges its authority. Anyone putting anything above the Bible or anyone degrading the Bible is not from God!

> *"You, dear children, are from God and have overcome them, because the one who is in you is greater than the one who is in the world. They are from the world and therefore speak from the viewpoint of the world, and the world listens*

to them. We are from God, and whoever knows God listens to us; but whoever is not from God does not listen to us. This is how we recognize the Spirit of truth and the spirit of falsehood." (1 John 4:4-6, NIV)

"But there will also be false prophets among the people, just as there will be false teachers among you. They will secretly introduce destructive heresies, even denying the sovereign Lord who bought them-bringing swift destruction on themselves." (2 Peter 2:1-2, NIV)

Life Study Lessons

1. *What is the meaning of "Counterfeit Christianity"?*

2. *How can a person tell if the scriptures in the Bible are being twisted?*

3. *Name some counterfeit Christian religions:*

4. *How does Satan use the scriptures to deceive you?*

5. *How did the devil use the scriptures to try to deceive Jesus in the wilderness?*

6. *How did the serpent deceive Eve in the Garden of Eden?*

7. *How can a person tell a true disciple of Jesus from a false one?*

8. *What are some of the false teachings infiltrating the body of Christ?*

9. *Name the beliefs of the "Statement of Faith" of your church:*

10. *When a church is teaching false doctrine, new revelations or strange manifestations what should you do?*

Chapter 6

In Dreams and Visions…

rom the time I was a child, until the age of 25, I had nightmares almost every night. In my dreams, demons would appear and try to posses or kill me. One night, at about 10 years of age, while I was sleeping, a demon spirit came to my room and stood in the doorway. I felt it coming closer and closer to me. I knew it wanted to kill me. I became paralyzed and could not scream or move. Nothing would come out of my mouth and I could not move my body. Even though I was not a Christian, I knew it was evil. When I awoke out of it I started to scream as loud as I could and my Uncle, who was in the next room, came and asked me what happened. I shared this with him but he just thought it was a bad dream. This experience and others I had while growing up, lead me into seeking for answers and opened me up to all types of false teaching. Half of my adult life, the search for the truth had led me to Jesus, the only begotten Son of God. After I became a Christian, I encountered many false teachings about dreams and visions.

In rare instances God will give instructions through dreams and visions. Today, a teacher, a pastor receives his message from the Word of God through study. The current trend of revelation operated by dreams, visions and prophecies entices numerous believers away from the truth in the already revealed Word of God.

Today, God speaks to us through the Bible. Please notice: "God, who at various times and in various ways spoke in time past to the fathers by the *prophets*, has in these last days [today] spoken to us by His Son." (Hebrews 1:1-2, NKJV) Jesus Christ is the living Word of God (John 1:1, 14), and the Bible is the Word of God in written form. God the Father gave it to Christ. Christ, in turn, inspired both the prophets and the apostles, and they preserved it for us (II Peter 1:21; Luke 1:70; John 16:13). The Father's will, commandments, and specific promises are revealed to us in the Holy Scriptures. God, then, is actually speaking to us through His Word, the Bible, which lays bare all of our agendas and brings us to Him as the source of ultimate truth as Hebrews 4:12 testifies: "For the Word of God is quick, and powerful, and sharper than any two edged sword, piercing even to the dividing asunder of soul and spirit, and of the joints and marrow, and is a discerner of the thoughts and intents of the heart." (KJV) So we must remember that God's Word is the final authority concerning the direction of our faith as Paul instructed the young pastor in 2 Timothy 3:16-17:

> *"All scripture is given by inspiration of God, and is profitable for doctrine, for reproof, for correction, for instruction in righteousness: That the man of God may be perfect, thoroughly furnished unto all good works." (KJV)*

So many people today are seeking for answers on TV, from talk shows or the latest New York Times Best-Seller by drawing upon their dream life or visions that provide profound direction for them. Many people claim to have dreams or visions that lead to teaching or experience that is contrary to God's Word. There are even others that teach how to interpret their dreams and even interpret dreams for others both in the secular and Christian worlds. I do believe God can speak through dreams. I also believe the Scriptures show that we can have dreams created out of our own thoughts (Ecclesiastes 5:3) or those inspired or influenced by the demonic (Deuteronomy 13:1-3). There are many in the Church who claim to have dreams or visions of heaven or hell. Even persons with visions or dreams that come to pass are not necessarily coming from God but are increasingly leading many astray—especially as we come closer to the return of Christ.

On examination the dreams, visions and revelations men receive can be divided into two groups. The first group would include the cult leaders of false religions that are clearly not doctrinally sound and whose revelations contradict the scripture. The modern day revelations of this group are clearly not from God, because God would never contradict Himself.

Often the "dreamer" is perpetrating a hoax intended to deceive people into following them. They claim their visions or visitations from God gave them special authority to form their new movements and teachings. A prime example is Joseph Smith, the founder of Mormonism, who claimed God and Jesus appeared to him and told him all the churches on earth were false. He was to form a new church and preach the "restored"

Gospel. However, the church he formed and its teachings are wholly unbiblical which proves Smith received no visitation from God. God does not contradict Himself.

The second group would involve those who have had experiences in which they believe God or Jesus appeared and spoke to them in a dream or vision. In the second group are also those who had strange, vivid dreams that left them very emotional. These people are very sincere. We can dismiss the revelations of the first group as being spurious, but what about the second group? These are people who profess to be Christians and are very sincere in believing or wondering if what they experienced was from God.

For example, many people in the Christian church are speaking and writing books about going to heaven or hell, speaking with Jesus, Mary and other prophets in a dreams and visions. There is no scriptural support for this experience. The problem with this type of encounter is that they take the experience that Paul had in 2 Corinthians 12:1-4 and justify their spiritual encounters. Let's break down what that means.

If you claim to visit anyone in heaven, it does not line up with the scriptures. Even if you speak to the prophets, the apostles or your deceased love ones. Paul's visit to the spirit world refutes the popular belief of spiritualism. Spiritualism is a modern form of infidelity with claims to communicate with the spirits of the departed. It is also claimed that information can be received by the living from the dead. This superstitious belief was called necromancy in the Old Testament. Paul made an actual visit to the spirit world, but he distinctly said that it was unlawful for him to reveal the things heard at that time. Being unlawful in his case it follows, therefore, that it is unlawful in any case for people to reveal to the living what they experience while absent from the body. In fact, Paul does not even claim to know exactly what had happened to him.

> *"I must go on boasting. Although there is nothing to be gained, I will go on to visions and revelations from the Lord. I know a man in Christ who fourteen years ago was caught up to the third heaven. Whether it was in the body or out of the body I do not know—God knows. And I know that this man—whether in the body or apart from the body I do not know, but God knows—was caught up to paradise and heard inexpressible things, things that no one is permitted to tell." (2 Corinthians 12:1-4, NIV)*

The only authentic instances of anyone communicating with us from the spirit world are found in the Bible, and only a very few people in all of human history were given this opportunity by God. In each case it was the result of a direct miracle initiated by God. When Elijah and Enoch were taken to heaven, they never returned. It is interesting how many people claim to have these experiences and are so detailed about it. Much money is given these people for their books and conferences to support their claims. If Paul was not permitted to tell, how can God change his mind with multitudes of people claiming to do so?

There is a danger when someone tells you to ask the Holy Spirit for dreams, visions, instead of focusing on learning the Word; it is a clear giveaway of what their intentions are. The Gnostic or mystic will always elevate dreams, visions, or a spiritual experience above the written Word. They will not question its authenticity because their belief is that there is no deception to be aware of. As one continues to become open and seek an "experience or new revelation" in this manner, instead of the literal written Word, new revelations can come more fluently through voices, dreams, visions etc. As they continually seek outside the Scriptures for their instruction, they eventually will deny the sufficiency of Scripture - and their spiritual health will suffer into deeper deception.

A dream and a vision are interchangeable. A dream is while we are sleeping and a vision is while we are awake. In fact, let's break this down and look at God's Word for the answer.

Bible Accounts...

Let's look at some examples. First of all, let's grasp the context of the time and place we are looking into...

In the year 604 B.C., in the city of Babylon and over the entire Babylonian Empire, reigned a king who was named, Nebuchadnezzar. This king had just finished spreading his empire to new regions because of many conquests, including Jerusalem, where he captured many of the Jews. Among these captured Jews was the young prophet Daniel. In the world at this time in history the power of this king, Nebuchadnezzar, was, without a doubt, totally undisputed. He was king of the world, to put it bluntly.

One night, the king had a very upsetting dream. When he awoke he was unable to remember the content of that dream. However, it still remained in his heart that it was a very upsetting thing he had dreamed. So he desired greatly to know what it was.

> *"Then the king commanded to call the magicians, and the astrologers, and the sorcerers, and the Chaldeans, for to shew the king his dreams. So they came and stood before the king." (Daniel 2:2, KJV)*

Nebuchadnezzar, like many kings of old, was accustomed to consulting astrologers and magicians, especially for the interpretation of dreams. However, this time, his demand was extremely unusual because of the fact that he was asking more than the simple interpretation of the dream: the king wanted to know everything about the dream including all that he saw in it even though he totally forgot the dream and its contents. Of course this troubled the magicians and astrologers greatly because they felt that it was completely impossible to tell the king what he had dreamed as well as the interpretation of it without knowing at least the dream itself.

> *"Then spake the Chaldeans to the king in Syriack, O king, live forever: tell thy servants the dream, and we will shew the interpretation." (Daniel 2:4, KJV)*

No different than today with all the psychics and magicians, the magicians and astrologers of Daniel's day were also fakes. These magicians and astrologers were in it for the money. It seems nothing really changes. These so called magicians and astrologers had no special power to see into the future or understand dreams. They were counterfeits, so as to make many believe they had this ability so as to fill their pockets. As today, it was a piece of cake to tell people what the dreams meant by merely giving bogus meanings that "appeared" to make sense to the hearer. No doubt, as today, demons were very beneficial in making some of the magicians and astrologers appear to be authentic by mixing truth with lies. The problem was, however, what the king was asking this time was totally different. He not only wanted the understanding of the dream. He wanted to know WHAT he dreamed as well! With that request, the king literally discovered he had employed nothing but a pack of liars and fakes as magicians and astrologers.

> *"But if ye will not make known unto me the dream, there is but one decree for you: for ye have prepared lying and corrupt words to speak before me, till the time be changed: therefore tell me the dream, and I shall know that ye can shew me the interpretation thereof." (Daniel 2:9. KJV)*

As we can see, the king's suspicions are confirmed when they could not comply with his request. Seeing how the magicians and astrologers could not guess his dream, he looked upon that as proof that they were nothing but fakes without any power whatsoever! Having been caught red-handed, they tried to pull the onus off of themselves by trying to tell the king that his demand was unreasonable, but it only made him even the more angry. The King was, in fact, so angry that he decided they should breathe their last breath for lying to him all those years.

> *"For this cause the king was angry and very furious, and commanded to destroy all the wise men of Babylon." (Daniel 2:12, KJV)*

The problem with this decree is Daniel was also considered one of the wise men because of his graphic faith in the one True God. He is a God who knows secrets. This death decree fell upon Daniel's head as well, so he quickly appeared before the king begging mercy so as to have time to do as he requested regarding the dream. Daniel wanted to ask the true God of Abraham to reveal to him the king's dream. Seeing how the king knew of Daniel, and his honest ways, he accepted his offer. Daniel immediately went to the Lord on this.

> *"Then was the secret revealed unto Daniel in a night vision. Then Daniel blessed the God of heaven." (Daniel 2:19, KJV)*

Daniel was blessed with the exact same dream the king had that night while sleeping. The Almighty Creator knows secrets as well as all dreams of mankind as well as any thought of the heart. So the very next day he rushed to the king to let him know what God had revealed.

"Daniel answered in the presence of the king, and said, The secret which the king hath demanded cannot the wise men, the astrologers, the magicians, the soothsayers, shew unto the king; But there is a God in heaven that revealeth secrets, and maketh known to the king Nebuchadnezzar what shall be in the latter days. Thy dream, and the visions of thy head upon thy bed, are these; As for thee, O king, thy thoughts came into thy mind upon thy bed, what should come to pass hereafter: and he that revealeth secrets maketh known to thee what shall come to pass. But as for me, this secret is not revealed to me for any wisdom that I have more than any living, but for their sakes that shall make known the interpretation to the king, and that thou mightest know the thoughts of thy heart." (Daniel 2:27-30,KJV)

The Lord blessed Daniel in a mighty way that day. As a true prophet of God always does, Daniel did not seek glory for himself. He made sure it was known that the secrets were revealed by God Himself so as to bless the king with knowledge of those things that troubled his heart as well as glorify the Lord. Had the magicians or astrologers known of this dream they would have sought glory for themselves so as to ensure further employment and "blessings" from the riches of the king.

"Thou, O king, sawest, and behold a great image. This great image, whose brightness was

excellent, stood before thee; and the form thereof was terrible. This image's head was of fine gold, his breast and his arms of silver, his belly and his thighs of brass, His legs of iron, his feet part of iron and part of clay. Thou sawest till that a stone was cut out without hands, which smote the image upon his feet that were of iron and clay, and brake them to pieces. Then was the iron, the clay, the brass, the silver, and the gold, broken to pieces together, and became like the chaff of the summer threshing floors; and the wind carried them away, that no place was found for them: and the stone that smote the image became a great mountain, and filled the whole earth."
(Daniel 2:27-30, KJV)

Daniel is blessed by the Creator with the exact same dream the king had so as to prove to the king there is a God that knows all secrets. Daniel is also blessed with the interpretation of this dream so as to further glorify the Lord as well as please the king at the same time. Such wisdom has this God we worship!

"This is the dream; and we will tell the interpretation thereof before the king. Thou, O king, art a king of kings: for the God of heaven hath given thee a kingdom, power, and strength, and glory. And wheresoever the children of men dwell, the beasts of the field and the fowls of the heaven

hath he given into thine hand, and hath made thee ruler over them all. Thou art this head of gold." (Daniel 2:36-38, KJV)

In the above passages, we can see that the Lord interpreted the dream and gave Daniel the entire dream! The King did not have to share one word. Let's take a look at Joseph's dream:

"Joseph had a dream, and when he told it to his brothers, they hated him all the more. He said to them, "Listen to this dream I had: We were binding sheaves of grain out in the field when suddenly my sheaf rose and stood upright, while your sheaves gathered around mine and bowed down to it." His brothers said to him, "Do you intend to reign over us? Will you actually rule us?" And they hated him all the more because of his dream and what he had said. Then he had another dream, and he told it to his brothers. "Listen," he said, "I had another dream, and this time the sun and moon and eleven stars were bowing down to me." When he told his father as well as his brothers, his father rebuked him and said, "What is this dream you had? Will your mother and I and your brothers actually come and bow down to the ground before you?" His brothers were jealous of him, but his father kept the matter in mind." (Genesis 37:5-9, NIV)

In these passages we can see that God gave Joseph a prophetic dream that later came to pass. Joseph himself was given the revelation of the dream and shared it with his brothers. God gave the dreams to Joseph to show him his purpose and for deliverance for him and his family. Even though the dreams were given, Joseph had no idea of how that was going to come about in his life or how God would orchestrate it. Many people that have dreams put much effort into believing they are real instead of believing God's Word.

God has given me many dreams through the years. Some of the dreams were warnings, some were demons attacking me, others were spiritual warfare, and even angels were in some protecting me from danger. Before I was a Christian, I did not realize that Satan had authority over my life. We are all God's creation but we are not all His children. I would have dreams about things when I was an unbeliever and they would come to pass. I now realize this was leading me into deeper spiritual deception. The danger in believing everything we dream is that we can be deceived. We must test and prove everything. How do we do that? We know by the scriptures and by the fruit of what it produces.

> *"Anyone who lives on milk, being still an infant, is not acquainted with the teaching about righteousness. But solid food is for the mature, who by constant use have trained themselves to distinguish good from evil" (Hebrews 5:13-14, NIV)*

The Lord speaks to every person differently. He knows how to communicate to each one of us as an individual so that we will understand what He is trying to say. There have been times I received a dream that was a warning and because I did not see any evidence of what was revealed to me, I ignored it and it cost me 10 years of almost complete destruction in my life. I now know better. I am not suggesting that He will speak to you in this way. Before I was a Christian, I had very vivid dreams and I believe this is a way where God speaks to me. At the same time, I also know the enemy has also deceived me through dreams.

I had a dream where I thought God showed me who my husband would be. God's presence in this dream was so powerful and familiar. I knew God's presence so I thought I could not be deceived. For 7 years I believed a lie. Finally I gave up on what I dreamed and asked the Lord to show me why I was deceived. How could this happen to a spirit-filled child of God? Then He showed me the scripture:

> *"Son of man, take up a lamentation upon the king of Tyrus, and say unto him, Thus saith the Lord GOD; Thou sealest up the sum, full of wisdom, and perfect in beauty." Thou hast been in Eden the garden of God; every precious stone was thy covering, the sardius, topaz, and the diamond, the beryl, the onyx, and the jasper, the sapphire, the emerald, and the carbuncle, and gold: the workmanship of thy tabrets and of thy pipes was prepared in thee in the day that thou wast created. Thou art the anointed cherub that covereth; and I have set thee so: thou wast upon the*

holy mountain of God; thou hast walked up and down in the midst of the stones of fire." (Ezekiel 28:12-14, KJV)

This is not an earthly king, as the word "cherub" is only used in references to angels. Lucifer was in the presence of God. He knows God's presence and I believe he can manifest a false presence or a false "anointing" that feels like God but which is not. That's why we need to test everything by the "fruit" it produces. This would include the fruit of the Spirit, the fruit of Righteousness and the fruit of Repentance. There is a growing movement of dream interpretation. There is nowhere in the Scriptures where there was a person who was teaching others how to interpret dreams. We are to only listen to the Lord and not to put our trust in man no matter how appealing it seems to our flesh, or else we will be lead into great deception.

"If a prophet or a dreamer of dreams arises among you and gives you a sign or a wonder, and the sign or the wonder comes true, concerning which he spoke to you, saying, 'Let us go after other gods (whom you have not known) and let us serve them, you shall not listen to the words of that prophet or that dreamer of dreams ; for the LORD your God is testing you to find out if you love the LORD your God with all your heart and with all your soul. "You shall follow the LORD your God and fear Him; and you shall keep His commandments, listen to His voice,

serve Him, and cling to Him. "But that prophet or that dreamer of dreams shall be put to death, because he has counseled rebellion against the LORD your God who brought you from the land of Egypt and redeemed you from the house of slavery, to seduce you from the way in which the LORD your God commanded you to walk. So you shall purge the evil from among you. (Deuteronomy 13:1-5, NASB)

God also speaks in dreams to warn us, as in Job 33, to keep man's soul back from the pit. An excellent example of this type of dream is mentioned in Matthew 27:19, where the wife of Pontius Pilate, the governor of Judaea, had a dream on the day of Jesus' trial before her husband—a dream which greatly distressed her. Though the contents of this dream are not disclosed in scripture there was something about it that caused Pontius Pilate's wife to be very fearful of her husband condemning Jesus—so much so that she urged him to have nothing to do with Jesus. This could very well mean she saw or heard something in her dream that was surely from God, in which she witnessed the consequences of her husband, Pontius Pilate, being condemned by God and sent to a godless eternity of conscious and physical torment in hell if he condemned Jesus. In this dream God probably told her or showed her that Jesus was a just and sinless man and, for that reason, she should urge her husband not to condemn Jesus so that he could avoid experiencing God's eternal wrath or to avoid going to the pit. God must also have wanted to make His warning to Pilate quite clear in the dream to Pilate's wife, because she said she had suffered not just some things but many things in the dream because of Jesus, and probably more if Pilate sentenced Him to death. The scripture reference in Matthew 27 of this dream to Pontius Pilate's wife from God that she relayed to her husband to keep him back from the pit, by refraining from condemning the innocent Son of God and Messiah Jesus who he was to try that day under Roman law is as follows:

"When he was set down on the judgment seat, his wife sent unto him, saying, Have thou nothing to do with this just man: for I have suffered many things this day in dream because of him. But the chief priests and elders persuaded the multitude that they should ask Barabbas, and destroy Jesus. The governor answered and said unto them, whether of the twain(two) will ye that I release unto you? They said, Barabbas. Pilate saith unto them, What shall I do then with Jesus which is called Christ (Messiah)? They all say unto him, Let him be crucified. And the governor said, Why, what evil hath he done? But they cried out the more, saying, Let him be crucified. When Pilate saw that he could prevail nothing, but that rather a tumult was made, he took water, and washed his hands before the multitude, saying, I am innocent of the blood of this just person: see ye to it." (Matthew 27:19-24, KJV)

Our final authority should always be based on sound Biblical doctrine. If our dreams cause us to backslide, rebel against the Lord in any way, serve other gods, fantasize, go back into the world or sin, we can already conclude that they are not from God. We should never put trust in anything except the written Word of God. As we grow and mature in Christ, hopefully, we will also learn from our mistakes. *"Yet in like manner these people also, relying on their dreams, defile the flesh, reject authority, and blaspheme the glorious ones."* (Jude 1:8, ESV)

The Lord your God proves you. God permits such impostors to arise to try the faith of His followers, and to put their religious experience to the test; for he who experimentally knows God cannot be drawn away after idols. The person who has no experimental knowledge of God may believe anything. Experience of the truths contained in the Word of God can alone preserve any man from Deism, or a false religion. They who have not this are a prey to the pretended prophet, and to the dreamer of dreams. (Clarks Commentary on the Bible)

Visions...

Within the charismatic movement, there are many who claim to have visions and it has become a dangerous phenomenon. A vision consists of something seen other than by ordinary sight. Throughout the centuries, mystics, prophets, and ordinary people from all religions have experienced visions from their deities or higher levels of consciousness that have informed them, warned them, or enlightened them. From

Genesis through Revelation, in the Bible, God uses visions and dreams as a principal means of communicating with His prophets and His people. In Numbers 12:6, God declares, *"...If there is a prophet among you, I, the Lord, make Myself known to him in a vision; I speak to him in a dream."* (NKJV) And in Joel 2:28: *"And it shall come to pass afterward that I will pour out My Spirit on all flesh; Your sons and your daughters shall prophesy, Your old men shall dream dreams, Your young men shall see visions."* (NKJV) Let's evaluate visions in the Bible and study about what the visions were and the purpose for them.

The Apostle Peter, even though he was a follower of Jesus, was in many ways still a devout Jew under the law. Among other things the law said that devout Jews should not have many dealings with the Gentiles, or people of the surrounding nations and that, if they could become God's people at all, they had to become Jewish proselytes or converts who were to keep the Law of Moses. Among other things the Law of Moses stated the Gentiles or people of the nations were unclean or defiled in God's sight because they didn't keep the Jewish dietary laws of the Law of Moses but instead ate unclean food on a regular basis. Peter's purpose was to continue to insist on the Gentiles becoming God's people according to the Law of Moses and denying them salvation or acceptance as children of the God of Abraham, Isaac and Jacob by God's grace alone and faith in Jesus the Messiah. God then sent this vision to Peter to turn him from his purpose by bringing a sheet with unclean animals or animals the Jews weren't allowed to eat under the Law of Moses and that the Gentiles were accustomed to eating, down to him and ordering Peter to kill them and eat them. This was God's way of saying that in the present and almost now finished Church Age (or Age of Grace) the Gentiles or people or the nations should be accepted also by Jewish believers in Jesus as full children of God without having to keep the Law of Moses, instead trusting in Jesus for salvation and living by the direction of the Holy Spirit.

The voice from God in this dream coming twice and the sheet coming down from heaven three times is an example that God sometimes has to repeat points in a dream to convince us of his message as it is mentioned in Job 33 about dreams. *God speaks once, yea twice but man perceived it not.* The scripture reference to God seeking to turn the Apostle Peter from his purpose of continuing to insist the Gentiles keep the Law of Moses, and not be saved and justified only by God's grace and faith in Jesus the Messiah or Christ by this vision of God ordering the Apostle Peter to kill and eat the unclean animals is as follows:

> *"On the morrow, as they went on their journey, and drew nigh unto the city, Peter went up upon the housetop to pray about the sixth hour: And he became very hungry, and would have eaten: but while they made ready, he fell into a trance and saw heaven opened, and a certain vessel descending unto him, as it had been a great white sheet knit at the four corners, and let down to the earth: Wherein were all manner of four footed beasts of the earth, and wild beasts, and creeping things, and fowls of the air. And there came a voice*

to him, Rise, Peter; kill, and eat. But Peter said, Not so, Lord; for I have never eaten any thing that is common (unholy) or unclean. And the voice spake unto him again the second time, What God hath cleansed, that call not thou common. This was done thrice: and the vessel was received up again into heaven." (Acts 10:9-16, KJV)

When a person wants to believe something they may very well have a dream or vision that tells them what they want. Then they begin to believe in their dream, considering it a spiritual revelation. This seems to be the basis for false dreams and false prophesy. Many dreams encourage us to follow the lust and passions of our flesh and lead us into deeper deception.

"For thus saith the Lord of hosts, the God of Israel; let not your prophets and your diviners, that be in the midst of you, deceive you, neither hearken to your dreams which ye caused to be dreamed. For the idols have spoken vanity and the diviners have seen a lie, and have told false dreams; they comfort in vain: therefore they went their way as a flock, they were troubled, because there was no shepherd." (Zechariah 10:2, KJV)

Testing the source

Test everything that claims to be supernatural. *"Do not put out the Spirit's fire; do not treat prophecies with contempt. Test everything. Hold on to the good. Avoid every kind of evil."* (1 Thessalonians 5:19-22, NIV)

If someone comes to you and says, "I've got a word from God" or "I had a vision and this is what I think God wants us to do", test it. That is what the Bible says. Test it. Don't put out the Holy Spirit's fire. Don't despise what is prophesied, but test everything. Go back and read Chapter 2. Hold onto the good and reject that which is evil.

Let me share a piece of advice with you. I believe that God can, and does, speak supernaturally today. Having said that, I offer this important caution: Do not ever make a major decision in your life solely on the basis of what you believe to be a supernatural experience. That is almost always a mistake. Don't get married because you had a vision. Don't go to college just because you had a dream. Don't move to China because you saw it floating overhead in the clouds. Don't kiss her or him just because the fish were kissing each other. You will get into trouble that way. Don't make a major decision in your life solely on the basis of that which appears to you to be supernatural.

Let's talk about a good test for anything that appears to be a supernatural message from God to you:

1. **The Test of Scripture.** Test it by the Word of God. Is it consistent with what God has said in his Word and sound doctrine? Does it reflect the character and nature of Jesus Christ? Will it lead me to a closer walk with God or further away from Him?

2. **The Test of Time.** Let's suppose you get a supernatural sign of some kind in a dream or a vision. It can come

from God or from Satan. Wait before you make a major decision towards that dream or vision. Wait a day. Wait a week. Wait a month. If it's from God, it will still be from God next week. If it's from God, it will still be from God a month from now. People get emotionally riled up because they think they've received a message from God. So they run out and do crazy things and ruin their lives.

3. **The Test of Counsel.** In the multitude of counselors, the Bible says, there is safety (Proverbs 11:14). God will rarely speak to you in such a way that no one else around you recognizes it as the voice of God. If it is truly of God, spiritual men and women normally will recognize it as well. That's the test of counsel. Deception often comes to lone rangers that have no accountability.

4. **The Test of Confirmation.** If you have a dream or a vision or some other unusual event that seems like a message from God, ask Him to confirm it by non-supernatural means. If it is from God, He will be glad to do that for you. And don't make a major decision about it until you have received that confirmation from other sources. There is a reason why He compares us to sheep and if you should decide to study sheep and their nature, you will know why.

Let's wrap this message up then with five practical conclusions. What are we going to do about dreams, visions, and supernatural signs? Here are five pieces of advice for you.

1. **Do not rule it out.**

    Although I tend to be very skeptical about many supposed supernatural revelations, I don't think we should go to the opposite extreme and rule them out altogether. I would hate for us to become so rationalistic in our faith that we said, "God, you can only speak to us this way. You can't speak to us that way." He's God. He can speak to us anyway he chooses. So don't rule it out.

2. **Do not seek it.**

    Don't seek supernatural signs (Matthew 16:4). This is where people get in trouble. They attempt to make common that which, by definition, is very rare. Many Christians never have a supernatural experience of any kind. It doesn't matter. You are not a less spiritual Christian if those things don't happen to you. God does not love you any less. He loves you just as much as He loves anyone else.

3. **Do not try to force God's hand.**

    Some people try to force God to give them a miracle. They think that by doing certain things they can cause God to respond in certain ways. "Lord, I'm going to fast until you send me a sign." It's always a mistake to try something like that. You may end up starving to death and the enemy loves these kinds of Christians. They become Satan's playground.

4. **Stay open to the Holy Spirit.**

    By that, I mean, stay open to the Holy Spirit's working in your life. He wants to guide your life moment by moment. Stay open to the Holy Spirit and let him guide you in any way he sees fit.

5. **Build your life on the Word of God.**

   Don't make the mistake of building your spiritual life on signs and wonders. God never meant for you to be a "miracle junkie," rushing from one emotional high to another. What will you do when the miracles stop coming? Or your dreams become ordinary? Or the clouds stop looking like Canada or Jesus? Or the fish stop kissing each other? Or the roofs no longer overhang the cabin walls? There are many experiences that seem as though they came from God but, in all actuality, they are from the devil himself disguised as an angel of light. Signs and wonders are going to be the primary way the anti-christ will deceive the inhabitants of the earth.

   "And he doeth great wonders, so that he maketh fire come down from heaven on the earth in the sight of men, and deceiveth them that dwell on the earth by the means of those miracles which he had power to do in the sight of the beast; saying to them that dwell on the earth, that they should make an image to the beast, which had the wound by the sword and did live." (Revelation 13:13-14, KJV)

There are many even today that are falling for deceptive visions and dreams and are preparing their hearts to be deceived by the anti-christ because they do not love the truth of God's

Word. There is only one solid foundation for you and that is the Word of God. Do not be led astray by dreamers and visionaries who want to lead you into basing your life upon dreamy impressions or compelling visions that lead you away from the authority of God's Word, which has spoken once and for all through Jesus alone. Anything else is an abomination to Him.

"Behold, I am against them that prophesy false dreams, saith the LORD, and do tell them, and cause my people to err by their lies, and by their lightness; yet I sent them not, nor commanded them: therefore they shall not profit this people at all, saith the LORD." (Jeremiah 23:32, KJV)

"And when this people, or the prophet, or a priest, shall ask thee, saying, What is the burden of the LORD? thou shalt then say unto them, What burden? I will even forsake you, saith the LORD. And as for the prophet, and the priest, and the people, that shall say, The burden of the LORD, I will even punish that man and his house." (Jeremiah 23:32-34, KJV)

"For in the multitude of dreams and many words there are also divers vanities: but fear thou God." (Ecclesiastes 5:7, KJV)

Life Lessons Study

1. *What is the difference between a dream and a vision?*

2. *Name several reasons why God spoke to someone in a dream or vision:*

3. *What purpose did God have for a man of God to interpret someone's dream?*

4. *Why is it dangerous for a person to learn dream interpretation?*

5. *How does a person test if the dream or vision is from God or the devil?*

6. *How can you tell if your dream is from God, your flesh, or the devil?*

7. *Share how a dream or vision has deceived you:*

8. *Share how a vision or dream has protected you from danger:*

9. *Who are some of the people, in the cults of our time, that received dreams or visions but were deceived:*

10. *Name some of the dreams or visions that happened in the New Testament:*

Chapter 7

In Ministry...

—⁓⚜︎⁓—

fter the Lord began opening doors for me in Christian ministry and television, I received an email from a worldwide major ministry asking me to come and sing. So I did. The man who invited me "was" a major part of that ministry for many years. He approached me as a godly Christian man and he said he very impressed with what I was doing in Christian and government arenas, including my love for God. He kept telling me about all the major ministers he knew (whom he did) and how much money he made in the ministry (ten million a year). After I sang for the event, he invited me to meet him for him for dinner. During dinner, he ignored me completely, but checked out other women and began talking with those at the tables around us. I was in shock, and I confronted him. He denied all of these behaviors even though that is what happened. Afterward, he took me to his home and tried to forcefully and aggressively have sex with me; was not about to take "no" for an answer. Thank God I was able to leave the situation without that happening. Before I left, he showed me all the knives, guns and military weapons he had. I came home extremely shaken up over the whole situation. I knew I could not expose him because the situation was too close to home and many of the people on Christian television knew him. He also told me about the things that go on behind the scenes with television evangelists whom he personally knew. I was appalled not only by what I heard, but that he was just as bad—and everyone knew it except me. Two people in ministry who knew him personally later told me that he is known for being a womanizer, a sex addict and a "player" who has many girlfriends. I was so embarrassed and wondered why no one had warned me of the harm and danger.

This experience is all too common in Christian ministry. Power and money control weak and vulnerable men, women and children. It has become common place for us to hear about the ministers who fall into sexual sin, rape, adultery, homosexuality, lavish spending habits and child molestation. When the church allows compromised Christian leaders to explain away sin, compromise truth, and sin with impunity, we exchange truth for lies. We become no better than idolaters—people whose credulous adoration of compromised leaders fulfill what Paul calls exchanging *"...the glory of the immortal God for images made to look like mortal man... exchanging the truth of God for a lie..."* (Romans 1:22, 25, NIV). The Story of King David, from 2 Samuel, is the tragedy of a man who believed the lie but, sadly, it represents a popular attitude in the Church today toward sin in Christian leadership. Unfortunately, although most Christians sincerely want truth and want to follow Biblical ethics, they too often listen to such lies from our leadership and instead of denouncing sin and demanding accountability we parrot excuses and allow compromised leaders to continue in leadership.

The objections against revealing a Christian leader's sin seem to imply that it is possible for one to have a valid Christian ministry or profession, and yet have a private life of corruption. However, the Bible explains that it is not possible for one's sinful conduct to have no negative effect on one's profession of godliness.

> *"To the pure all things are pure, but to those who are defiled and unbelieving nothing is pure; but even their mind and conscience are defiled. They profess to know God, but in works they deny Him, being abominable, disobedient, and disqualified for every good work." (Titus 1:15-16, NKJV)*

Attempting to combine immorality with godliness to produce spiritual fruit is completely contrary to scriptural teaching. In fact, Paul ranks it with "profane and vain babblings" and warns Timothy to avoid "contradictions of what is falsely called knowledge" (1 Tim. 6:20). It is unethical for Christians to cover up for leaders who have achieved their position through false qualifications or stories, or who are living immorally. Can the church claim a higher ethical standard than the world when we adopt a "code of silence" worthy of the most pernicious organized crime conspiracy or even some suspected invisible satanic ring?

My new name for this kind of deception is "the Christian mafia". I have seen many of these evils over and over again. It is as though people are mesmerized with leaders even though they are aware of the evil that comes through them and their lifestyle. It is as though a person literally does not want "to know" about the wickedness of an individual and pretends either that it doesn't exist or that it is none of their business. From women and men sexually propositioning me, reports of rape among the pastors with boys and women, to completely sexually impure lives; it must break the heart of our God.

Unfortunately, I have experienced divorce. I had been a Christian for about 6 years at the time. It was a long time ago but I will never forget the experience I had with Christian pastors and ministers. My ex-husband had been physically abusive and had been charged multiple times by the police for abusing me. I was asked to stay with him until the pastor of the church I attended told him that he could no longer have me stay with him because it could cost me my life. The state issued a "no contact order" for two years stating my ex-husband could have no contact with me in any form, and scheduled a court date for trail regarding his stalking and physical abuse. On that day, as I walked into the court house, my pastor looked at me and said, "What a shame", specifically because I told the police, and because my ex-husband was to be prosecuted. I walked into the side room with the police and prosecuting attorneys and just cried knowing that my own pastor was "ashamed" of me. During the trial, not only did the pastor lie but said that I was the abuser, and not my ex-husband. I never thought I would see the day a pastor blatantly lie while knowing the truth. Other pastors lied during the trial as well. I was astonished and devastated at the same time. They had no regard for my life or well being. Most of all, they had no fear of God. This story is all too common as well. Through years of being in ministry, I have heard horror stories from multitudes—and experienced some myself, as well.

> *"What sorrow awaits you teachers of religious law and you Pharisees. Hypocrites! For you are like whitewashed tombs—beautiful on the outside but filled on the inside with dead people's bones and all sorts of impurity. Outwardly you look like righteous people, but inwardly your hearts are filled with hypocrisy and lawlessness." (Matthew 23:27-28, NLT)*

Call Them Out

Paul writes Titus that it is the responsibility of the church to hold the leader accountable for his sin: *"Wherefore rebuke them sharply, that they may be sound in the faith"* (Titus 1:13, KJV). Paul also commands Christians to rebuke sinning leaders publicly: *"Those who are sinning rebuke in the presence of all, that the rest also may fear"* (1 Timothy. 5:20, NKJV). Paul took his own advice, as recorded in Galatians 2, and publicly rebuked Peter "before them all" (v.14).

If we neglect to uncover sin within the church, we rob the church of the integrity it should expect from its members. The church becomes weak through compromise, and the leader becomes weak because of his or her immorality. Fallen leaders betray the trust of those they lead. Maturity in the Lord, which is an essential part of qualifying one for spiritual leadership, can be confirmed only by an established pattern of resisting sin and walking faithfully with God, family, and others.

1 Thessalonians 5:21-22 commands us to "test all things," and Paul commended the Bereans for "searching the scriptures" to test what he himself had taught them (Acts 17:11). The Christian whose life is characterized by truth telling must support spiritual leaders whose lives exemplify Christian maturity, and must hold those leaders accountable. If a Christian leader is chosen whose life is bound by immorality, the Christian has the obligation then to expose that sin publicly since the leader is public and his actions impact the church he leads. The old saying, "What one does not know won't hurt him", is as far from the truth as good is from evil. God even warns the Church in Hosea 4:6 that His "people will be destroyed for a lack of knowledge". Because of ignorance, which is a lack of knowledge, people do things they don't know will harm them, and when they do obtain knowledge, often the damage has already been done. Misinformation results in people doing things they believe to be correct based on the "wrong" information. Unfortunately, this too results in harm and consequences that can't be changed.

Good discernment and moral accountability should be practiced among believers. The Old Testament establishes this pattern. Instructions concerning false prophets in Deuteronomy 13:1-5 assume the prophet arises from the congregation of Israel. The passage admonishes the people to banish idolatry from their families, "If your very own brother, or your son or daughter, or the wife you love, or your closest friend" (v. 6). Deuteronomy 13 instructs the Israelites how to practice good discernment within their own communities: "you must inquire, probe and investigate it thoroughly". If the community is idolatrous, it must be dealt with publicly (v. 14). Psalm 50:18 states that one who sees a crime and doesn't report it has moral culpability.

The New Testament continues the theme of good discernment within the believing community, most notably when the Bereans test Paul's teachings (Acts 17:11) and the Thessalonians are commanded to test all things (1 Thessalonians 5:21-22). Judgment is not excluded, but unrighteous judgment is, as Jesus declared: "Stop judging by mere appearances, but instead judge correctly." (John 7:24, NIV)

Jesus expelled the money changers from the temple, denounced the Pharisees and scribes, and rebuked the teachers of the Law. He reprimanded Peter in front of the other disciples (Matthew 16:22-23). Paul followed Jesus' example and named false teachers in the church (2 Timothy 2:14-19) and openly criticized Peter (Galatians 2:11-14).

Paul warned that false teachers would arise within the church; "Even from your own number men will arise and distort the truth in order to draw away disciples after them." (Acts 20:30, NIV) The false teachers of Jude are said to "have secretly slipped in among you." (Jude 1:4)

Christians are sometimes uncomfortable with criticism within the Church because they wrongly assume that public criticism, because it is painful, is also destructive. On the contrary, the "pain" of biblically conducted confrontation produces individual growth (1 Timothy 4:16), encourages others to Christian maturity (1 Timothy 5:19-20), promotes Church strength (Ephesians 4:15), and preserves the Church's reputation in the world (1 Peter 2:12).

Each one of us should examine our own hearts. We shut our eyes to evil done in the church and pretend that it will go away. If we allow this to go on without any justice and truth, we are guilty by association. Yes, guilty of the same sins.

"Son of man, I have made you a watchman for the house of Israel; so hear the word I speak and give them warning from me. When I say to the wicked, 'O wicked man, you will surely die,' and you do not speak out to dissuade him from his ways, that wicked man will die for his sin, and I will hold you accountable for his blood. But if you do warn the wicked man to turn from his ways and he does not do so, he will die for his sin, but you will have saved yourself. "Therefore, son of man, say to your countrymen, 'The righteousness of the righteous man will not save him when he disobeys, and the wickedness of the wicked man will not cause him to fall when he turns from it. The righteous man, if he sins, will not be allowed to live because of his former righteousness If I tell the righteous man that he will surely live, but then he trusts in his righteousness and does evil, none of the righteous things he has done will be remembered; he will die for the evil he has done. And if I say to the wicked man, 'You will surely die,' but he then turns away from his sin

*and does what is just and right—if he gives back
what he took in pledge for a loan, returns what
he has stolen, follows the decrees that give life,
and does no evil, he will surely live; he will not
die." (Ezekiel 33:7-15, NIV)*

Discipline

The first person to whom we must be accountable is God
Himself, but he also says we should submit ourselves to one
another. Jesus gave us the ultimate example of submission
when he became obedient to the cross, and when he washed
his disciple's feet, but I feel like there's more to it than service
to one another. I don't really know how to explain it... but, as
it says in Ephesians 5:21, submit yourselves to one another out
of reverence for Christ.

The consequences of compromising Biblical truth and
ethics are devastating. Like an insidious cancer, lies and
immorality eat away at the church. Tender believers lose their
faith, the associates of the sinner fall into sin themselves, and
unbelievers mock the church and reject the Gospel. While covering up for a compromised leader or tolerating sin in the midst
of the congregation may appear at first glance to be loving,
compassionate and "good", it is like a disease which cannot be
seen—but we see the results.

We cannot condone continuing sin within the church or ministries. We must expose it, deal with it Biblically, call sinners
to repentance, and then extend the forgiveness, discipleship,
restitution, and restoration offered from God's Word. We must

recognize sin as sin and be determined, by the grace of God, to live up to the potential He has set for us. The church can't bring God the glory He deserves as long as the present level of ignorance is tolerated in the church and as long as we continue to embrace evil practices. A national survey by the Barna Group among people who describe themselves as Christian and involved in a church discovered that only 5% indicated that their church does anything to hold them accountable for integrating Biblical beliefs and principles into their life.

Accountability is one of the means God uses to bring about solid growth and maturity with the freedom to be what God has created us for but the problem is that we live in a society that has become very individualistic. The prevailing attitude is to be your own man or woman, do your own thing, be your own boss, and often this attitude is promoted or stated in a way that undermines accountability to God and others. The Bible in no way denies our individualism. Indeed, it promotes it, but in a way that holds us each accountable to one another. Proper individualism leads to a certain amount of inventiveness, ingenuity, and freedom, but it can also breed license and irresponsibility without accountability. The fact is you can't make disciples or produce growing and mature Christians without accountability.

We are talking about teaching, exhorting, supporting, and encouraging one another in such a way that it promotes accountability to Christ and to others in the body of Christ, but never by manipulation or domination.

There are numerous New Testament passages which teach the concept of accountability of the flock to the leaders (e.g., 1 Thess. 5:12; 1 Tim. 3:1-5; Heb. 13:7, 17; 1 Pet. 5:2-3) The need for accountability goes beyond the leadership and falls into the realm of the "one another" concept of the New Testament.

*"submitting to one another out of reverence for Christ." (*Ephesians 5:21, *ESV)*

Firstly, it should be noted that "submitting" is the fourth in a series of adverbial participles. These can be detected in most translations by words that end in "-ing" beginning with verse 19. These participles are best understood as expressing the results of the filling by means of the Spirit (vs. 18). Submission, which certainly includes accountability, is applied to the whole body of Christ as a Spirit-produced and mutual responsibility to promote obedience to Christ. In the same way, you who are younger, be subject to the elders. And all of you clothe yourselves with humility toward one another, because God opposes the proud but gives grace to the humble.

In 1 Peter 5:5, we again meet with the word "hupotasso." Here it is applied to younger men with older men of wisdom. But if accountability is going to work, there must be genuine humility toward one another. Further, accountability with humility is related to humbling ourselves under God's authority—its goal is becoming accountable to God.

In a good family, discipline should be overwhelmingly instructive and encouraging. Teaching a child how to make his bed by patient instruction is part of a well disciplined home. Nevertheless, spankings (especially in the younger years) will probably be a needed part in an atmosphere of loving, patient instruction and admonition.

So it will be in the church. Mutual accountability should be mainly instructive and affirming. It means that all of us in the church are responsible both to give and receive encouragement, counsel, consolation, exhortation, and admonition (1 Thessalonians 5:14; Hebrews 3:13; Galatians 6:1; 1 Corinthians 1:3).

This is implied in the precious doctrine of the priesthood of all believers (1 Peter 2:5, 9; Revelation 1:6; 5:10). We are priests for each other in that we minister God's grace to each other (1 Peter 4:10), intercede for each other with God (Romans 15:30), and confess our sins to each other (James 5:16). Membership in the church then is a commitment to the tender love of encouragement, and the tough love of confrontation—to give it humbly and to receive it without defensiveness.

Only in rare cases does the New Testament suggest that accountability will lead to the all-church, disciplinary act of ex-communication. This kind of discipline results when a member forsakes the covenant and persists in a refusal to forsake and repent of willful sin. Such cases seem to be ones in which the sin of a member is open for the public to see and is impenitently persistent. In other words, the commitment to pursue obedience is broken. Instead of pursuing obedience, the member has settled into a behavior or an attitude with no effort to flee from it as sin. This would be a willful decision to live in violation of the covenant.

Let us, as Christians, make every effort to not only confront an individual or ministry when they are opposed to the Word of God and causing great damage but let us also gently restore a person once they have come to "true repentance." Too many pastors and evangelists are living in sin and when they are caught, soon afterward, return to ministry. I believe there should be a time period of at least one year of proven discipline, integrity, accountability, counseling, growth and change before a person is allowed to go back into the ministry again. Otherwise, they are more than likely to repeat their evil. Some sins are so devastating that I believe some leaders should never be placed in any leadership position ever again. Unfortunately, there is a growing trend in Christian ministry where most leaders have no accountability to anyone above their position. The dangers are imminent not only to false teaching but also to all kinds of secret evil behind the scenes. How often we are watching on television screens across the nations about ministers and ministries that have been exposed of doing evil and bring shame and disgrace to the Gospel and the body of Christ.

New believers should also be tested in their life, conduct, service, fruit, etc...before they should be allowed to take a leadership position in a church or ministry over a period of a long time. Many people who are appointed too quickly to ministry leadership roles cannot hold up to the test of time of true integrity, character and holy living.

> *"Never be in a hurry about appointing a church leader. Do not share in the sins of others. Keep yourself pure." (1 Timothy 5:22, NLT)*

Life Study Lessons

1. *What, if anything, do you see in your own church that may demonstrate a compromising of the truth?*

2. *How does my own sin affect others around me?*

3. *In what ways do I hold leadership to a higher standard than I hold myself?*

4. *What does being a "hypocrite" mean?*

5. *Explain the ways in which your pastor or leader is accountable to others?*

6. *Share some stories in how your pastor or leader has an excellent reputation?*

7. *In what ways do you inadvertently support corrupt leaders?*

8. *What is the pattern according to the Word of restoring fallen leaders?*

9. *What should your response be to an unrepentant leader?*

10. *How does God feel towards those leaders that fall before the sinners?*

Chapter 8

In Signs and Wonders...

*J*was at an event where there was a special guest speaker. I had never heard of him but I trusted my friends who were pastors and evangelists and had invited me. During the church service, I heard this special guest speaker sing in what they call the "prophetic". Then he spoke for a few minutes and asked people to pray and ask God for gold teeth. So we all did. He asked people to get up from their seats and walk around the room and expected a manifestation. I felt uncomfortable and left the service for a while. When I came back towards the end of the service, I saw strange manifestations. People were screaming, shaking and going crazy with excitement saying they had received gold teeth. Others were jerking and rolling on the floor. I just stood and watched. We were told by the speaker to check each other's mouths for gold teeth and people told me to open my mouth and they said I had gold teeth. I ended up having dinner with the speaker and other leaders afterwards for 2 hours. The speaker pulled out a 52-karat ruby ring and others gems and showed them to me. He said the angel "Emma" gave these to him. I asked questions for hours such as, "Why would God*

*do this?", though I never got a solid, biblical/doctrinal expla-
nation. Nevertheless I was still quite impressed and excited
about my experience. In the days and months to follow, I told
everyone about my experience! I had never seen or encountered anything like it.*

Jesus warns us in the Bible about the deception in the end
times. Deception is hard to detect. When we have wonderful
experiences in the supernatural, we immediately believe they
are from God. We never would imagine in a million years that
they could be coming from Satan himself.

> *"For false messiahs and false prophets will rise
> up and perform great signs and wonders so as
> to deceive, if possible, even God's chosen ones."
> (Matthew 24:24, NLT)*

After this experience, I began traveling across the United
States speaking and singing in churches and crusades. I
encountered even more interesting experiences. I ministered
in a church where the pastor prayed for people and I saw
miraculous healing before my eyes. I was so excited. I even
experienced a supernatural encounter where I began to laugh
uncontrollably as he prayed for me. After the service that pastor
told me that he goes to heaven on a regular basis and receives
teachings from Samuel the prophet. Each night I was booked
to minister in worship for the entire event. One afternoon in
particular, several leaders from Washington and Oregon met
for lunch. I also went along. One of the leaders in a prayer
movement pulled out bags of gemstones. There were diamonds,

rubies, onyx and all types of precious stones. She said they had appeared in her home and church at various times. She also spoke about gold dust that appears on her hands, face and skin all the time.

Another pastor and his wife, sitting at the other end of the table, shared how God transports them physically to two locations at once. This man gave me a book which he wrote about how to experience this and other signs and wonders. They also shared with me the dangers of not discerning what is from God and what is not.

At this point, I was pretty convinced. I was really impressed but, at the same time, I thought that I must not be as close to Jesus as I should be. I was questioning myself as to why I was not experiencing these signs and wonders as these others within the church. I had heard about these signs and wonders throughout most of my Christian walk, but I could never relate to them. It seemed too deep for me and I could not understand a lot of the Christian "lingo" by which they would speak and teach, so I left it alone. Now God was allowing me to come face to face with it.

A lot of the language, experiences, and teachings reminded me of the New Age beliefs. Since I was a child, I was taught how to connect to God by becoming one with Him. I always believed that God needed us and it was not until I became a Christian that I realized the opposite was true. We need Him.

As I began to research these manifestations, I realized that many religions not only have the same manifestations, but they also encourage everyone to seek the experiences. An example of current trends that signs and miracles validate one's teaching is William Branham, one of the original and greatest evangelists of the post-World War II Healing Revival. Branham worked astounding miracles of healing in his crusades. His gifts of supernatural knowledge of those to whom he ministered remains unparalleled, even among modern healing evangelists of today. Despite all of his gifts, however, Branham's doctrine was always marginal at best, and towards to the end of his ministry, it became outright heretical. He denied the doctrine of the Trinity, teaching instead the "Jesus only" doctrine. He taught that he was the prophet Elijah, whose ministry would result in the return of Jesus. There were even pockets of his followers who believed that he was not only a prophet, but also the incarnation of Jesus himself. Although Branham's is an extreme example, it illustrates that a ministry of miracles and healing in no way proves soundness of doctrine.

I became a Christian in 1990 and, for 16 years of ministry, I have seen and heard of these manifestations. In fact, I have also been involved with a lot of these ministries as a guest solo artist or a speaker. Ignorance is the best way to describe my lack of knowledge on this subject.

> *"My people are destroyed for lack of knowledge. Because you have rejected knowledge, I also will reject you from being priest for me. Because you have forgotten the law of your God, I also will forget your children." (Hosea 4:6, NKJV)*

So we see here that we can be "destroyed" for the lack

of knowledge. Being destroyed means to completely ruin, demolish, break up, defeat completely, and crush or to render useless or ineffective.

> *"As for prophecies, they will pass away; as for tongues, they will cease; as for knowledge, it will pass away. For we know in part and we prophesy in part, but when the perfect comes, the partial will pass away. When I was a child, I spoke like a child, I thought like a child, I reasoned like a child. When I became a man, I gave up childish ways. For now we see in a mirror dimly, but then face to face. Now I know in part; then I shall know fully, even as I have been fully known."*
> *(1 Corinthians 13:8-12, ESV)*

In the meantime, knowledge is needed because there are problems as a result of "The Fall." Knowledge that is true allows problems to be solved and avoided. If a car breaks down, mechanical knowledge is useful, otherwise it is unnecessary. It is the same with all of life's problems. God gives us knowledge to help "fix" broken people, protect ourselves from the difficulties of life, and allow love to express itself in good works.

> *"To one there is given through the Spirit the message of wisdom, to another the message of knowledge by means of the same Spirit."*
> *(1 Corinthians 12:8, NIV)*

Scripture often uses the words *knowledge*, *understanding*, and *wisdom* interchangeably, but occasionally they are spoken of as separate and distinct. Thus, it may be useful to attempt to define the differences of meaning. Knowledge relates to facts. Understanding is the ability to lift the meaning out of the facts, and wisdom knows what to do next. Since God rarely gives all three gifts to any person, we need to cooperate and assist each other with our particular gift in this area along with those that have gifts in other areas. Let's talk about how to discern which miracle or sign is from God and which is not.

These signs shall follow...

Claims of miracles occurring at services (or in distant countries where they cannot be verified) are multiplying and becoming more and more wildly unbelievable all the time. Those who do not accept second hand accounts of miracles giving no names or facts are derided as lacking in "faith," refusing to believe what does not fit "their own tradition," or of "putting God in a box." A "cessationist" has become a dreadful thing to be labeled. It is amazing to see how many succumb to this peer pressure and check their minds at the mention of the word "miracle." Yet, so far, there have not been any medically verified, true, supernatural, biblical miracles as a whole; it is pretty much the traditional faith healing story, with most claims concerning those ailments most susceptible to emotional influence, as in all the religions and systems of thought centered on producing healings.

*"And these signs will follow those who believe:
In My name they will cast out demons; they will
speak with new tongues; they will take up serpents; and if they drink anything deadly, it will
by no means hurt them; they will lay hands on
the sick, and they will recover." (Mark 16:17-
18, NKJV)*

As Jesus said, "These signs shall follow". We are not
supposed to seek after signs but they will follow those who
believe. What are the signs? Casting out demons, speaking
with new tongues, deadly serpents, drinking poison and
laying hands on the sick and they will get well. So if we
look at what is happening in the church and other religions,
it should sound an alarm in our hearts. In fact, most of the
signs and wonders that are happening have nothing to do
with deliverance. I have seen different religions having healings, exorcisms, signs and wonders. One of the dangers is
that even though it seems like it's from God, it only opens
the door for the demons (evil spirits) to attached themselves
to an individual.

*"When the unclean spirit is gone out of a man,
he walketh through dry places, seeking rest,
and findeth none. Then he saith, I will return
into my house from whence I came out; and
when he is come, he findeth if empty, swept,
and garnished. Then goeth he, and taketh with
himself seven other spirits more wicked than*

himself, and they enter in and dwell there: and the last state of that man is worse than the first. Even so shall it be also unto this wicked generation." (Matthew 12: 43-45, KJV)

When God did any type of sign, wonder or miracle in the Old Testament—and all the way through the New Testament—he always had the purpose of salvation and/or deliverance. He never did anything to show off. In fact, there was never any element of any substance left behind from the heavenly realm into the earthly realm. Manna was fed to the children of Israel and it ceased after they tasted the good of the land.

"The manna ceased on the day after they had eaten some of the produce of the land, so that the sons of Israel no longer had manna, but they ate some of the yield of the land of Canaan during that year. (Joshua 5:12, NASB)

In many of these religious meetings, manna is appearing and no one is questioning it. Instead, the people are thrilled and believe these things are coming from God. They have no idea that the enemy of their soul has seduced them. When God did a sign or wonder, he used the natural elements that already existed to accomplish the purpose for which he intended. Let's take a look at examples of these:

1. **Many signs and wonders occurred in the time of the Old Testament.**

   a. The sun stood still at Joshua's command.
      Joshua 10:12-14

   b. Water flowed from a rock when Moses struck it.
      Exodus 17:5, 7; Psalms 78:15-16, 20

   c. The Red Sea parted so that God's people could cross.
      Exodus 14:22; Hebrews 11:29

   d. An iron ax floated on water.
      2 Kings 6:5-6

   e. The waters were turned to blood.
      Exodus 7:17

   f. The dead were raised to life.
      Hebrews 11:35

   g. The son of the widow of Zarephath.
      I Kings 17:17-23

   h. The Shunammite's son.
      2 Kings 4:32-37; 8:1, 5

   i. The young man laid in Elisha's sepulcher.
      2 Kings 13:2

j. Aaron 's rod blossomed.
    Numbers 17:1-9

k. The three Hebrew children in the fiery furnace remained
    unharmed.
    Daniel 3:23-27

l. The widow's cruse of oil and barrel of meal was con-
    tinually replenished during a time of famine.
    1 Kings 17:9-16; 2 Kings 4:2-7

m. Baalam's ass spoke.
    Numbers 22:23-30

n. Jonah, swallowed by a whale, was vomited up alive
    after three days in its belly.
    Jonah 1:17; 2:10

o. Moses' rod became a serpent; his hand became tempo-
    rarily leprous when he put his hand in his bosom.
    Exodus 4:3-4, 30; 7:10, 12

p. The Jordan parted when Elijah "smote the waters" with
    his mantle.
    2 Kings 2:8

q. The sun went backwards (so to speak).
    2 Kings 20:9-11

r. Manna fell from the sky to feed God's people.
   Exodus 16:4-31; Psalms 78:24, 25

s. Gideon's fleece became wet and dry according to his request concerning the word of the Lord to him.
   Judges 6:36-40

t. Elijah pronounced a drought upon the land, *"and it rained not on the earth by the space of three years and six months. And he prayed again, and the heaven gave rain ... "*
   I Kings 17:1, 14; 18:41-45
   James 5:17-18

2. Many signs and wonders occurred in the time of the New Testament.

a. Jesus Himself performed many mighty signs and wonders among the people.
   John 20:30; 21:25; Acts 4:30

b. Jesus changed water into wine.
   John 2:1-11

c. Jesus walked on water.
   Matthew 14:22-33; Mark 6:42-52; John 6:16-21

d. Jesus took money from the mouth of a fish.
   Matthew 17:24-27

e. Jesus fed the multitudes with a few loaves and fishes.
    Matthew 16:8-10

i.The five thousand.
    Matthew 14:15-21; Mark 6:35-44;
    Luke 9:12-17; John 6:5-14
ii.The four thousand.
    Matthew 15:32-39; Mark 8:1-9

f. Jesus cursed a fig tree, and it shriveled up.
    Matthew 21:17-22; Mark 11:12-14, 20-24

g. Jesus told the storm to cease, and it became silent.
    Mark 6:45-52

h. At Jesus' word the dead were raised to life.

i.The widow's son.
    Luke 7:11-16
ii.Jairus' daughter.
    Matthew 9:18-19, 23-26; Mark 5:22-24, 35-43;
    Luke 8:41-42, 49-56
iii. Lazarus.
    John 11:1-46; 12:9

i. At Jesus' command his disciples brought in a draught of
    fish where there had been none.
    John 21:5-12

3. The early church experienced many miracles as well.

> *Acts 2:43;4:16; 5:12; 14:3; Romans 15:19;*
> *2 Corinthians 12:12*

a. Those bitten by poisonous snakes remained unharmed.

> *Mark 16:18; Luke 10:19; Acts 28:3-6*

b. Those imprisoned for the gospel's sake escaped unharmed.

> *Acts 5:17-25:12:1-17:16:25-40*

c. Those upon whom just the shadow of Peter fell were made whole.

> *Acts 5:15*

d. *"And God wrought special miracles by the hands of Paul, so that from his body were brought unto the sick handkerchiefs or aprons, and the diseases departed from them, and the evil spirits went out of them."* (Acts 19:11-12 KJV)

e. The dead were raised to life.

i.Peter raised Dorcas (Tabitha).
> *Acts 9:36-40*

ii.Paul raised Eutychus.
> *Acts 20:9-12*

However, it must be recognized that Satan can also perform lying signs and wonders. Not everything supernatural is of God.

- Exodus 7:9-11; 8:17-19
- Deuteronomy 13:1-5
- Matthew 24:24
- Mark 13:22
- 2 Thessalonians 2:9
- Revelation 13:13-14; 16:14; 19:20

Now that we have read the examples of God and His purposes, we can clearly understand that He always had a purpose in the end for every sign, wonder or miracle He did. We can also see that He never brought anything out of the heavenly realm into the earth to leave behind any elements in any of these examples in scripture. Gold dust, angel feathers, manna, gold nuggets, gems, etc., are not coming from God. The leaders and spectators involved in this signs, wonders and miracles movement argue that either God is doing a "new thing" or He is just blessing His people. There is no scriptural support for these types of manifestations. The Word of God is twisted and sound doctrine has no room in the life of a person that is open to deception. God clearly warns us that He will send strong delusion in the end times. Satan is preparing the way for these individuals to not only worship the beast and his image, but also to be deceived by his signs and wonders.

> *"And then if anyone says to you, 'Behold, here is the Christ'; or, 'Behold, He is there'; do not believe him; for false Christs and false prophets will arise, and will show signs and wonders, in order to lead astray, if possible, the elect. (Mark 13:21-22, KJV)*

Why will God send them strong delusion? Because they did not have a love for the truth of God's Word. Paul wrote of this attitude telling how some would perish.

> *"Because they received not the love of the truth, that they might be saved. And for this cause God shall send them strong delusion that they should believe a lie. That they all might be damned who believed not the truth..." (2 Thessalonians 2:10-12, KJV)*

These false prophets are controlled by seducing spirits; and while working under the guise of end-times preachers, pastors, teachers, elders, and church laymen they are preaching, teaching and promoting doctrines of devils.

> *"Now the Spirit speaketh expressly, that in the latter times some (Christians) shall depart from the faith, giving heed to seducing spirits, and doctrines of devils;" (1 Timothy 4:1, KJV)*

To clarify; the strong delusion will not be sent by God solely because of the actions of the false prophets, or due only to the blasphemous content of their false teachings, but also the strong delusion will be sent upon those who claim to be Christian and are proven apostate due to their acceptance of ungodly teaching. The Strong Delusion will be sent upon the false teachers and those who believe them. The seducers in the Christian church today are those who have gained good reputation, perhaps through pseudo-biblical teachings, but afterward, having betrayed the Holy Word of Jesus and the sound Biblical doctrine entrusted to them, have turned away from the Truth entirely.

Under the prompting of evil spirits these seducers have now begun teaching heresy and error compounded; of which Jesus said are "doctrines of devils". Ignoring the clear scriptural warning of being cursed for adding to or taking away from God's Holy Word, today's false prophets are foolishly, and to their own eternal destruction, teaching a new and different gospel.

Heart of God

The God of Abraham, Isaac and Jacob is not only all powerful, but full of justice and mercy. He loves us even while we were or are sinners. Whichever category we find ourselves in, we can be assured that He never gives up on us. Even until the end of our last breath. There are strong guidelines that He gives us to protect us from deception. The root of all deception begins with us.

People seem to be drawn to the miraculous and let their emotions lead them astray. Many today assume that if it is supernatural it must be the Lord, but do they ever, in their excitement, stop to consider the message given and how it compares with Scripture? I think the answer in many cases today is, probably not.

"Not everyone who says to Me, 'Lord, Lord,'
shall enter the kingdom of heaven, but he who

does the will of My Father in heaven. Many will say to Me in that day, 'Lord, Lord, have we not prophesied in Your name, cast out demons in Your name, and done many wonders in Your name?' And then I will declare to them, 'I never knew you; depart from Me, you who practice lawlessness!'" (Matthew 7:21-23, NKJV)

Coming on the scene is a false religion that will try hard to appear to be Christian but, in reality, will be the doctrine of demons. This doctrine will likely be that we are all 'little gods' working towards becoming 'enlightened' which is the doctrine of the New Age movement but is also the false doctrine many "Christian" teachers are promoting today. God warns us throughout the Bible of this great deception that is not only coming but already at work in our time.

I believe some of the chasing after signs and wonders Word of Faith teachers are already hard at work laying the ground work for the Anti-Christ and False Prophet. We are given instructions in the Bible not only to run from these false teachers, but also to expose them.

"I urge you, brothers, to watch out for those who cause divisions and put obstacles in your way that are contrary to the teaching you have learned. Keep away from them." (Romans 7:16, NIV)

"Beloved, when I gave all diligence to write unto you of the common salvation, it was needful for me to write unto you, and exhort you that ye should earnestly contend for the faith which was once delivered unto the saints." (Jude 1:3, KJV)

"Them that sin rebuke before all, that others also may fear." (1 Timothy 5:20, KJV)

"This witness is true. Wherefore rebuke them sharply, that they may be sound in the faith;" (Titus 1:13, KJV)

We know and understand that sound doctrine is our safe guard against all deception. Experiences can be extremely deceptive especially when they are not mentioned anywhere in the scriptures. If our final authority is not the Bible, then there is no foundation for judging the "truth" from a "lie". Most of the false supernatural experiences that people have are justified through the twisting of the scriptures. Those individuals never stay in context with what is written. They pull pieces out of the written Word to justify their beliefs. We are never to do that and that is precisely why spiritual deception occurs. Most Christians want to receive those things that the Lord is doing that are miraculous, however some of the so-called miracles of God are not coming from Him at all, but are glorifying men and not God. As Christians we cannot receive nor accept all miracles, signs and wonders just because the words "God" or the "Bible" are attributed as being the source of those things.

The Bible tells us in 1 Thessalonians 5:21: *"Prove all things; hold fast that which is good."* (KJV)

What should our role as Christians be in regard to the acceptance of a sign, miracle or wonder? We are told to *prove all things*, not to reject them because they might be strange or new to us. However, we should not receive them either, until we *prove* them. Most Christians do not study or even read the Bible. How do we *prove* things? All true Christians are in agreement that our standard is the Word of God, the Bible. God left us this Book as a reference, benchmark, or gauge so we could know whether something is good or evil, truth or error, right or wrong.

> *"All scripture is given by inspiration of God, and is profitable for doctrine, for reproof, for correction, for instruction in righteousness: That the man of God may be perfect, thoroughly furnished unto all good works." (II Timothy 3:16-17, KJV)*

Not only are we to test or try the spirits in men, but we are to do the same with any supernatural manifestations that we might experience. Today, when the world is being exposed to so many false things we need to be careful not to expose our spirits to false dreams, visions, revelations, prophecies, voices, signs, miracles, wonders, etc. The Word of God definitely teaches that God can manifest Himself in any, or all, of the above things; yet we are not to accept everything that comes in the name of Jesus. We need to test or prove these also. One of Satan's greatest devices is to counterfeit the real things of God and come to us disguised as the working of the Holy Spirit, and at others times he will come as an "angel of light" in signs and wonders.

> *"And then shall that Wicked be revealed, whom the Lord shall consume with the spirit of his mouth, and shall destroy with the brightness of his coming: Even him, whose coming is after the working of Satan with all power and signs and lying wonders, And with all deceivableness of unrighteousness in them that perish; because they received not the love of the truth, that they might be saved. And for this cause God shall send them strong delusion, that they should believe a lie." (2 Thessalonians 2:8-11, KJV)*

The greatest miracles are those God does in people's personal lives. Start with salvation. To come out of darkness into the light is truly a miracle. God also does more miracles in our lives beside salvation. He solves problems, brings blessings, and sets people free. He moves and works. Some of those things are miracles of the supernatural, but many of them are of the seemingly natural but, nevertheless, they are just as supernatural, and from God.

Life Study Lessons

1. *What is the difference between a sign and a wonder?*

2. *What was the purpose of a sign or a wonder?*

3. *Name five signs or wonders found in the Old Testament:*

4. *Name five signs or wonders found in the New Testament:*

5. *How do we test a sign or wonder to know if it is from God or Satan?*

6. *What would you do if a sign or wonder did not line up with sound doctrine but happened to you?*

7. *What are some of the ways we will be deceived in the end times?*

8. *What are some of the signs and wonders the devil will perform to deceive us in the end times?*

9. *What has been the greatest miracle in your life?*

10. *Share the signs and wonders the magicians did during Moses' time:*

Chapter 9

In the Appearance…

─◦◦⚬✠⚬◦◦─

everal years ago, someone close to me shared a story. She said: I was a sheep upon a mountain that was full of green pastures and rolling hills. As I looked around the rolling hills, there were also other sheep grazing with me. As I turned, I saw the Great Shepherd tending to His sheep. He began to lead the sheep further up the mountain. As I was preparing to go along with the other sheep, I heard a rustling coming from the bushes in front of me. In my curiosity, I drew closer to the bushes as I turned and saw the other sheep leaving to the Shepherd's leading. When I got to the bushes, a wolf dressed in sheep's clothing jumped out at me and growled like an angry lion. I was so frightened that it paralyzed me full of fear. The face of the wolf was still visible even though it was dressed like a sheep. All of a sudden, the wolf stop growling and I was astonished at its appearance. It became a beautiful wolf. I was completely mesmerized by the beautiful nose and its hair finely combed. Its eyes became like dove's eyes. The wolf looked so kind and gentle. While I was in the state of a trance and completely taken by its beauty, it all of a sudden became a vicious frightening wolf again.

It was growling at me with such fierceness. When I became paralyzed and full of fear again, it turned back into the beautiful wolf with a mesmerizing beautiful face. This went back and forth several times. All of a sudden, I felt the rod of the Shepherd hitting the side of my leg. He was leading me back to the flock. Then I heard His voice. I knew my safety was with the other sheep of His pasture—the body of Christ.

How many times have we looked at someone's face and they appeared innocent, full of love and looked joyous? As humans we are drawn to children, puppies, nature, innocence, etc., however, the question at hand is, should we judge a book by its cover? I was astonished that, in that story, she was mesmerized when the wolf became a beautiful—but it was still a dangerous wolf! Have you ever met a person who seemed so pure in their eyes and so sweet in their countenance yet turned out to be cunning and crafty beyond your wildest dreams? Let me share another example from my own life.

Being in ministry was not something that I imagined God had planned for me. I remember there was one point in my life when women seemed to be flocking to get close to me. One, in particular, became a good friend of mine. She was beautiful, sweet, giving, and very involved in ministry. We became very close and I thought I had known everything about her. One night we were out to dinner and one of her male friends happened to be there. When she went to the restroom, he began to share of how he and my girlfriend met on a regular basis for illicit sex. I listened but I was in shock. After that evening, I found out from others that she had many men with whom she engaged in this lifestyle. I never thought in a million years that she would ever live that lifestyle especially since she was in Christian ministry. I have run through countless men and women who live this way and you would never be able to tell by meeting them "face to face."

Many of us judge a person by their sweet face, and smile. Some of us judge a person by the hardness of their face and of not smiling at all. When we meet someone, we observe the way they are dressed, the way they talk, walk, and what not. Those observations "help" us in making a judgment (right or wrong) about the person. I have found that people perceive an introvert as arrogant, while a person who sweet-talks is considered extremely friendly or a "*good*" person. People also make judgments about someone's status/wealth from what they wear and what they don't.

When I first began to attend church, I remember I would wear short, mini-skirts and clothes that were inappropriate. Thank God that people treated me with so much love. If that had not happened, I may not have become a Christian. On the other extreme, we have people that are dressed holy on the outside, but are not good on the inside. Jesus said in Matthew 23:28 *"In the same way, on the outside you appear to people as righteous but on the inside you are full of hypocrisy and wickedness."* (NIV) When someone's sweet face is framed in an attractive and appealing physical symmetry—face, body, height and physical build that sets them apart in the crowd as a beautiful or handsome individual—they draw a far greater degree of influence and attention than an average person.

TRUTH THROUGH YOUR EYES...

If we examine our decisions based on our perceptions of a person or an event, it can be potentially deadly to us spiritually—and even physically—if we allow a seductively appealing perception to cloud our judgment rather than sound verifiable proof. It is easy to see evil when it is exposed in front of us, but can our perception of someone's outer appearance also be deceptive? What about the wolf that is dressed in sheep's clothing or the false prophets and christs that will gain our attention in the end times? Since this book is focusing on deceptive beauty, we will stay focused on that. Does the devil come in looking evil or good, beautiful or ugly? There must be a foundation on how to judge good from evil that is not based on personal perception, but of truth drawn from scriptures.

Let's talk about beauty on the spiritual level. Many people are claiming to see the appearance of Jesus in the flesh, face to face, or even in the clouds. There are also so-called prophets, teachers and pastors that are teaching gullible Christians how to have this encounter. Let the alarm sound! In fact, Jesus warned his disciples in Matthew 24:23-24, *"Then if anyone says to you, 'Behold, here is the Christ,' or 'There He is,' do not believe him. For false Christs and false prophets will arise and will show great signs and wonders, so as to mislead, if possible, even the elect."* (NASB)

If you begin to see the appearance of manifestations that are not doctrinally sound in God's Word, then run! If anyone teaches other than the Word of God, it is false teaching. Those who have the Holy Spirit in them will hear God's Words. They will consent to wholesome words. Those who do not know God, will not consent (John 8:47).

Many people take scripture out of context to validate their personal experiences, and what they see with their eyes. The Lord Jesus warned in Matthew 24:23: *"Then if anyone says to YOU, look here is the Christ! or 'There! Do not believe them."* (NKJV) I do believe that Jesus can appear in someone's dream or in a vision, but NEVER in the flesh. *"No one has ever seen God; but if we love one another, God lives in us and his love is made complete in us."* (1 John 4:12, NLT) Jesus made it absolutely clear he would come the same way he left and that he will get the church collectively. There should be no debate on this matter.

We make many judgments on an individual's appearance — whether they are pure or impure — even by what a person's clothes look like.

> *"And the same John had his raiment of camel's hair, and a leathern girdle about his loins; and his meat was locusts and wild honey." (Matthew 3:4, KJV)*

When John grew up, God called him to be a preacher and reformer. But John was no well-dressed, "feel good" preacher. He lived in the wilderness and ate grasshoppers and wild honey. He wore primitive clothing of camel's hair with a leather belt. The description of John is brief and stark. The "hair" cloak might have been a rough fabric woven from camel's hair, or a camel skin itself. The text is ambiguous. It was, however, quite reminiscent of the adornment of certain Old Testament prophets (Zech. 13:4), particularly Elijah, who, as we have noted, foreshadowed John (2 Kings 1:8). Jesus once said: *"John came neither eating nor drinking, and they say, He has a demon"* (Matthew 11:18, KJV). "Eating and drinking" stood for socializing. The prophet was not a party-goer. His ascetic life-style appeared almost demonic, like those possessed of evil spirits who apparently frequented the desolate areas (Mk. 5:2-3). He did not seek out the multitudes; rather, somehow, he attracted them. John's message of "repentance" entailed a deep consciousness of offense to God within the sinner's heart, with a required reformation of life. When he saw superficial Hebrews submitting to his immersion, void of any radical change of conduct, he rebuked them: *"You offspring of vipers, who warned you to flee from the wrath to come? Bring forth, therefore, fruit worthy of repentance"* (Matthew 3:7-8, KJV). THIS IS LOVE. John bluntly told people they would suffer the wrath of God if they did not change their ways. Yet, when John preached, people felt that God was working among them, and huge crowds of people went into the wilderness to listen to him.

John announced that the kingdom of God was coming near. He warned the people that being God's chosen people was not enough to save them from God's wrath. They must repent and change their sinful ways. He warned the well-to-do that they must share their food and clothing with the less fortunate. He exposed the greed of tax collectors and warned them not to cheat people. He warned soldiers to be satisfied with their wages and not take advantage of people. John criticized King Herod for unlawfully marrying his brother's wife. This confrontation eventually led to John being beheaded on the king's order.

I am sure if John the Baptist appeared to you, while eating wild locusts and honey and living in the wilderness, would you know what you see? How about James 2:2? *"Suppose a man comes into your meeting wearing a gold ring and fine clothes, and a poor man in shabby clothes also comes in. If you show special attention to the man wearing fine clothes and say, "Here's a good seat for you," but say to the poor man, "You stand there" or "Sit on the floor by my feet," have you not discriminated among yourselves and become judges with evil thoughts?"* (NIV) How about John 7:24, where Jesus says, *"Stop judging by mere appearances, and make a right judgment."*

When a person does not make a righteous judgment according to the Word of God and His grace, he or she becomes "legalistic". In Christianity, legalism is the excessive and improper use of the law (i.e., the Ten Commandments, holiness laws, etc.). This legalism can take different forms. The first is where a person attempts to keep the Law in order to attain salvation. The second is where a person keeps the law in order to maintain his salvation. The third is when a Christian judges other Christians for not keeping certain codes of conduct that he thinks need to be observed. This kind of legalism, where a Christian keeps certain laws and regards other Christians who do not keep his level of holiness with contempt, is a frequent problem in the church.

Now, I want to make it clear that all Christians are to abstain from fornication, adultery, pornography, lying, stealing, etc. Christians do have a right to judge the actions of other Christians in these areas where the Bible clearly speaks, but in the debatable areas we need to be more careful. This is where legalism is more difficult to define. Romans 14:1-12 says that we are not to judge our brothers on debatable issues. One person may eat certain kinds of foods where another would not. One person might worship on a particular day where another might not. We are told to let each person be convinced in his own mind (Rom. 14:5) and our freedom should never violate the scriptures.

TRUTH THROUGH HIS EYES

Jesus warned us that in the end times, there would be great delusion. Stephen's face in the book of Acts looked like an angel, while at the same time we are warned of wolves looking like sheep. In Galatians 1:8, Paul said, *"But though we, or an angel from heaven, preach any other gospel unto you than that which we have preached unto you, let him be accursed."* (KJV) Yet, in Rev 14:6,7, John says, *"And I saw another angel fly in the midst of heaven, having the everlasting gospel to preach unto them that dwell on the earth, and to every nation, and kindred, and tongue, and people Saying with a loud voice, Fear God, and give glory to him; for the hour of his judgment is come: and worship him that made heaven, and earth, and the sea, and the fountains of waters."* (KJV)

Anyone reading the context of that passage would quickly understand that the angel in Revelation 14 is not accursed. Angels were always involved in revelation to mankind. Paul, under prophetic inspiration, warns the believers then, and us, now, of receiving new understanding from a spiritual source that would alter what was first delivered to them. Today so much gets blamed on the Holy Spirit with teachers speaking heresy from the pulpits.

To "pervert" something means to twist a thing around and to destroy it by having additions to grace, distorting the nature of the person and the work of Christ.

To anathematize someone is to label them a false teacher. If someone teaches another Gospel that affects who Christ is, or how one relates to Him, or distorts grace by subtracting or adding any work it becomes another Gospel. They are to be cut off, cast away. Anathema—a thing devoted to God without hope of being redeemed. In the Old Testament, if it was an animal, it was to be slain. In the New Testamen it is person or thing doomed to destruction. There are many angelic visitations that I have heard about in our century. These manifestations have become very dangerous. Most of these are not angels but demons. We must also take into account that angels in the Bible always appeared as male and never female. Everything must be tested by the Word of God. The angels can look sweet and holy, but they can deadly and counterfeit.

> *"And no marvel; for Satan himself is transformed into an angel of light. Therefore it is no great thing if his ministers also be transformed as the ministers of righteousness; whose end shall be according to their works." (2 Corinthians 11:14-15, KJV)*

In fact, there are people whom I have met who have a beautiful countenance, a glowing face and exude a type of love, but they are following a false religion, a counterfeit Christian religion or no religion at all. As I have traveled and been in ministry for the past 16 years, I have also been deceived by this. How many times have we, ourselves, appeared holy and righteous, but we knew it was fake. I can remember the times I knew I was disobedient to God but I had a sweet smile on my face and a holy glow in front of others. We hide because we do not want people to know who or what we really are. If our secret lives were put on a screen, each one of us would be pronounced guilty and labeled as deceivers! Not one of us could escape.

We can also be self-deceived. How many times do we follow a teacher or get into a relationship because their countenance and face is beautiful or their flattering words and teaching are lovely to us. These examples I have mentioned are seen through "our eyes". We are also shown in the end times, that there will be great signs and wonders that will be seen by "our eyes" and "felt" by our experiences. The only way we can keep from being deceived is to know the truth of the Word of God and solid doctrine (teaching). When Jesus looked at a man or a woman, He was able to see their heart. We are not able to see someone's heart. We are only to judge their fruit. Jesus said that every tree will be known by its fruit—not at face value. *"Make a tree good and its fruit will be good, or make a tree bad and its fruit will be bad, for a tree is recognized by its fruit."* (Matthew 12:33, NIV)

> *"But the fruit of the Spirit is love, joy, peace, longsuffering, gentleness, goodness, faith, meekness, temperance: against such there is no law."* *(Galatians 5; 22-23, NIV)*

195

"And this is my prayer: that your love may abound more and more in knowledge and depth of insight, so that you may be able to discern what is best and may be pure and blameless until the day of Christ, filled with the fruit of righteousness that comes through Jesus Christ—to the glory and praise of God." (Philippians 1:9-11, NIV)

"Produce fruit in keeping with repentance." (Matthew 3:8, NIV)

"Do not judge according to appearance, but judge with righteous judgment." (John 7:24, NASB)

"And He will delight in the fear of the LORD, And He will not judge by what His eyes see, Nor make a decision by what His ears hear; But with righteousness He will judge the poor, And decide with fairness for the afflicted of the earth; And He will strike the earth with the rod of His mouth, And with the breath of His lips He will slay the wicked." (Isaiah 11:3-4, KJV)

So in the scriptures, we see that the Lord judges righteously. We are to ask Him to give us discernment to do the same. He does not want us to be deceived by what we see whether it is a person, a manifestation, or an angel. I have personally been deceived on all three levels. I have also witnessed others being deceived by what they see or their perception of what they see. I will stress again that everything must be judged according to God's Word and sound doctrine. We must only behold the beauty of the Lord.

> *"O worship the LORD in the beauty of holiness: fear before him, all the earth." (Psalms 96:9, NKJV)*

Now that we have discussed the natural and spiritual examples this deception, we can examine our lives and identify the countless times that we have been deceived. Men and women have a tendency to be drawn to their natural senses. We will get more into that in the next chapter. If they "look" beautiful, holy, or pure, it does not mean they really are. Remember what the apostle Paul warned us about in 2 Corinthians, that Satan's angels transform themselves into angels of light and his servants as ministers of righteousness. Remember to test the "fruit".

"Therefore it is no great thing, etc." Meaning it is not to be a surprise. You are not to wonder if people of the basest, darkest character put on the appearance of the greatest sanctity, and even become prominent as professed preachers of righteousness.

"Whose end shall be, etc..." Their doom in eternity shall not be according to their fair professions and plausible pretences, for they cannot deceive God; but shall be according to their real character, and their works. Their work is a work of deception, and they shall be judged according to that. What revelations there will be in the day of judgment, when all impostors shall be

unmasked, and when all hypocrites and deceivers shall be seen in their true colors! And how desirable is it that there should be such a day to disclose all beings in their true character, and forever to remove imposture and delusion from the universe! (Albert Barnes' commentary notes on the Bible)

Life Lessons Study

1. *How have I ever judged a person's appearance?*

2. *How have I been deceived by a person's appearance?*

3. *In what way have I deceived another person by appearing innocent?*

4. *Should I rely on my senses or the Word of God when I judge another person or both?*

5. *How is my behavior affected when I meet someone or encounter something that is beautiful?*

6. *How is my behavior affected when I meet someone or encounter something that is unattractive?*

7. *What is the meaning of "a wolf in sheep's clothing"?*

8. *How do I perceive my own appearance?*

9. *How does my perception of beauty affect my spiritual and natural judgment?*

10. *How is my natural and spiritual perception consistent with sound biblical doctrine?*

Chapter 10

In the Senses...

During the late night hour, I shut myself away seeking the Lord in prayer. I began to cry out to Jesus for more of His presence. As I lay on the floor, I was so engulfed in His presence and weeping. He began to give me revelation of the war of the flesh and the spirit. He showed me within my own members, there was a war inside of me. I saw how much my flesh hated God and the Holy Spirit living inside of me loved God. I felt the hatred and the love inside of myself as if there were two different people. It was war—a literal war—between the flesh and the spirit inside of me! Galatians 5:17 says, "The sinful nature wants to do evil, which is just the opposite of what the Spirit wants. And the Spirit gives us desires that are the opposite of what the sinful nature desires. These two forces are constantly fighting each other, so you are not free to carry out your good intentions."

Our body has five senses; taste, smell, touch, hearing and sight. How dangerous to use these senses to judge moral law and spiritual laws! Although they are created by God for His glory, let's look at an example of how these senses can lead us astray.

"When the woman saw that the tree was good for food, and that it was a delight to the eyes, and that the tree was desirable to make one wise, she took from its fruit and ate; and she gave also to her husband with her, and he ate." (Genesis 3:6, NASB)

There is a saying, "If it feels good, do it". We are driven by the lust of the eyes, the lust of the flesh and the pride of life. As a woman in ministry, I have encountered this problem on many levels. One night, I was scheduled to sing at a large concert. A few minutes before I went on the stage, the main musician who was supposed to play the piano approached me. He told me that if I did not go out with him that night after the concert, he would not play for me. I was left stranded. Ultimately, God came through. The number of men in ministry who have propositioned me for sexual favors is countless. Even bi-sexual and homo-sexual behavior has become common place and accepted in many venues and denominations. This is not excluding women who seduce men. It became so disheartening for me that I actually stepped away from singing for about 3 years. It was nothing different than the world.

How many times have we chosen mates or friends by their appearance, our sexual appetite, or because they had something that we want for our personal benefit and selfish desires? There are also ministries that chose people to represent them based only on their appearance. I love the scriptures that tell about David being chosen by God. In 1 Samuel 16, I was looking at the scriptures of Samuel coming to Bethlehem to find the man whom God had chosen man to take Saul's place as leader or king of Israel. It is interesting to note that Samuel was given an assignment by God even while Samuel was mourning over the fact Saul had lost his leadership role. In verse 7, after Samuel has introduced himself to Jesse and told them that he wanted to sacrifice with them, we find the LORD gives instruction to Samuel again. *"But the LORD said unto Samuel, Look not on his countenance, or on the height of his stature; because I have refused him: for the LORD seeth not as man seeth; for man looketh on the outward appearance, but the LORD looketh on the heart."* (KJV)

Samuel was just like any other man. Even though he was a prophet who followed the LORD'S instruction, he was still a man that looked upon a man's countenance. Countenance, in the Hebrew, means appearance, whether handsome, looks, etc. It's always amazed me that men would look upon a man's worthiness by his outward appearance or first impressions. Man has no right to judge a person by his looks.

We usually make our judgments based upon what we think we see and perceive, but what we often do not realize is that what we are focusing on and seeing may be just what we know (our knowledge!) and not God's Knowledge. We ought to discern whether a person is full of the fruit of Life from the tree of Life and know that this is the ONLY thing which is vital—Christ and His Life. We typically misjudge by instead judging from our own knowledge of good and evil—thus we make our judgments and decisions based upon what WE believe to be either good or evil. Our enemy still deceives us in the same way as he deceived Adam and Eve: by tempting us to make a judgment about something, and then deceiving us into believing our judgments and perceptions are correct and that they will not bring death!

The truth will only bring life when it is given in Jesus Christ and according to His Word. In giving any judgments, we have to be very careful and sure that we are sharing only what HE wants us to and thus allowing His Spirit to bring further revelation in His own time and way to the person. Otherwise we may be stepping ahead of Him and taking over the role of the Holy Spirit in a person's life and bringing unnecessary offense and division as a result. We are not called to be "Holy Spirit junior."

We need to be looking for Christ's Life in one another and uniting on that one thing instead of nit-picking over 'many things'. When we judge one another based upon our knowledge, we are likely to be unintentionally judging God's work. For example, you may see someone who appears to be open and trusting and decide that they are naïve, having never had their trust betrayed, when the exact opposite may be true. Their trust may be the result of the Life of Christ which has triumphed in enabling them to continue to trust in spite of that trust having been abused! You may know someone who is strong and unshakeable, and conclude that they are proud, stubborn, arrogant and un-teachable. Yet, you may be completely wrong. What you may not see is that this strength is the result of the work of Christ, which came about through much weakness, humbling and brokenness; God's strength, which we have mistaken as natural strength. In judging these things incorrectly based upon our limited knowledge we have, in fact, judged the fruit and work of the Tree of Life in their lives.

Who are we to criticize and judge God and His work in someone? We need to instead discern and know LIFE! The Hebrew word for *Life* means something which is *flowing, fresh, active, alive, sustaining* and *maintaining*. His Life must be what we discern, perceive and focus upon.

We like how the fruit tastes, we like how it looks and ultimately we become wise in our own eyes. After speaking with pastors and leaders, it seems the biggest cause for divorces is pornography. Lust is exploding and our society is becoming desensitized. Even the large majority of single men and women who are Christian do not life a sexually pure life. A person that does not know Jesus is expected to live in darkness—He or she has not come to the Light of the World—but the person who claims to know Jesus is commanded by the Lord to live sexually pure.

> *"And you were dead in your trespasses and sins, in which you formerly walked according to the course of this world, according to the prince of the power of the air, of the spirit that is now working in the sons of disobedience. Among them we too all formerly lived in the lusts of our flesh, indulging the desires of the flesh and of the mind, and were by nature children of wrath, even as the rest." (Ephesians 2:1-3, NASB)*

I am astonished at how many people I have had a chance to minister to about their addictions to pornography, sex, drugs, alcoholism, abuse, bitterness, money, fame, un-forgiveness, and the list goes on. Some people are sincere about deliverance while others will just drain the people who will listen to them with no desire for deliverance. When we see our sins as God sees them, it causes us to tremble. Many people have lost the fear of the Lord. When disobedience sets in, we open the doorways to spiritual deception. Our church pulpits are full of leaders who want to tickle our ears. The whole Gospel is not preached because they fear losing large tithe payers or offending the hearers. They fear the people more than they fear the Lord.

"Then Saul said to Samuel, 'I have sinned. I violated the LORD's command and your instructions. I was afraid of the people and so I gave in to them.'" (1 Samuel 15:24, NIV)

Saul blamed his sin on the people instead of his own covetousness. He wanted to spare the best cattle for himself. The Lord rejected Saul from being the king over Israel.

When a person gives in to disobedience, deception sets in unless that person is quick to repent. If not, it is very difficult to convince them of the truth. Deceived people do not believe they are deceived. They need the power and mercy of God to reach them. A person in deception may walk in sexual sin and still believe they are right with God. They are unable to give up their sexual appetite because it "feels" right. We are to put no confidence in the flesh.

THE TREE OF THE KNOWLEDGE OF GOOD AND EVIL

God put the tree of knowledge of good and evil in the Garden of Eden to give Adam and Eve a choice to obey, or disobey, Him. Adam and Eve were free to do anything they wanted, except eat from the tree of knowledge of good and evil. *"And the LORD God commanded the man, 'You are free to eat from any tree in the garden; but you must not eat from the tree of the knowledge of good and evil, for when you eat of it you will surely die.'"* (Genesis 2:16-17, NIV) God gives commands for different reasons. Some of His commands reflect absolute moral principles (e.g., "Do not commit adultery"). Other commands are given to specific individuals in specific situations. For instance, God's commandment to Noah to build an ark doesn't apply to the rest of us, nor does it mean that shipbuilders and sailors are holier than those who stay on land. God's command to Adam and Eve was not a command to avoid all knowledge, nor was it a command to all of humanity to avoid learning about morality.

It was the command God chose to give in order to test Adam and Eve, to give them a free choice whether to obey him or not. If God had constructed the Garden of Eden so that there were no rules and no way for Adam and Eve to do wrong, then Adam and Eve would have been effectively forced to obey God. In order for us to be free—which in this case refers to the freedom to follow or ignore God—we have to be able to make choices. Adam and Eve couldn't have chosen to follow God if they literally had no other choice.

The Adamic fallen nature (of sin that resides in us all) desires to become the "god" of self. We desire to control our life, others and our circumstances. All of the world's pleasures become enticing and desirable. The fallen nature of man cannot desire the things of God. In fact, it is at war with God. Each one of us apart from Jesus desires to become a "God". We may deny it, but we prove it in our actions. We choose through our God-given free will to choose life or death, blessings or a curse. Our nature, apart from God, is to run our own lives in our own way. Each of us, as human beings, worship something. It is in our nature to do so. When you hear a person say "I will" over and over again, it is a pretty good indication they are the "god" of their lives. Observe how it contrasts to what Jesus said: *"Father, if You are willing, take this cup from me; yet not my will, but yours be done."* (Luke 22:42, NIV)

We must be careful never to judge by the external by what we think we see, but by what we are shown by the Spirit of God.

> *"You set yourselves up to judge according to the flesh and by what you see. I do not set Myself up to judge or condemn anyone. Yet even if I do judge, My judgment is true; for I am not alone in making it, but there are two of us, I and the Father Who sent Me. I have much to say about you and to judge and condemn. But He Who sent Me is true and I tell the world only the things that I have heard from Him."*
> *(John 8:15, 16, 26)*

We cannot justify judging our brothers and sisters by what we observe in the natural as if the Bible gives license to that; but balance is required because by the same token we must not avoid having to judge when it is necessary and required.

According to Paul, we are not required to pass judgment on the world, but rather on those who are *part of us*! We normally do the opposite; we judge those who are of the world who are "so much worse than us" which is such pride, self righteousness and hypocrisy on our part! It seems we wouldn't dare speak out against the sin that is in the Body; but Paul seemed to do the opposite:

> *"I'm not responsible for what the outsiders do, but don't we have some responsibility for those within our community of believers? God decides on the outsiders, but we need to decide when our brothers and sisters are out of line and, if necessary, clean house." (1 Cor 5:12, 13)*

Your Ways, Not Mine

Many people have already judged themselves simply by accepting or rejecting the Word of God.

> *"Anyone who rejects Me and persistently sets Me at naught, refusing to accept My teachings, has his judge; for the very message that I have spoken will itself judge and convict him at the last day." (John 12:48, AMP)*

*"Jesus said, I came into this world for judg-
ment, as a Separator in order that there may be
separation between those who believe on Me and
those who reject Me, to make the sightless see
and to make those who see become blind. Some
Pharisees who were near, hearing this remark,
said to Him, Are we also blind? Jesus said to
them, If you were blind, you would have no sin;
but because you now claim to have sight, your
sin remains. If you were blind you would not be
guilty of sin, but because you insist, We do see
clearly, you are unable to escape your guilt."
(John 9:39-41, AMP)*

We must ask the Holy Spirit to reveal those areas in our
lives where we do not see clearly or are completely blind. This
is one area in which our brothers and sisters can be very helpful
in helping get the speck (or beam!) out of our eye. When we are
looking in the mirror of the Word we can only see one side of
ourselves; sometimes others can show us things which they can
see which we are not able to see ourselves, but it must be in the
Way, the Truth and the Life of Christ or it will bring destruction
to a person. Our enemy delights in accusing and condemning
us by pointing out all our faults and getting us occupied with
analyzing ourselves and trying to make "self" better or more
acceptable. It cannot be done. There is nothing in us naturally
that is right and holy, which is why we so desperately need
Christ to redeem us; not only from sin but also from self! May
He give us grace to be willing to see and receive His judgment

on our own flesh and to exercise righteous judgment from Him.

Until we ask Jesus into our hearts, we are unable to desire to do the will of God. Jesus said we must be born again to enter into the kingdom of heaven. The Lord said, *"And I will give you a new heart, and a new spirit I will put within you. And I will remove the heart of stone from your flesh and give you a heart of flesh. "I will put My Spirit within you and cause you to walk in My statutes, and you will be careful to observe My ordinances."* (Ezekiel 36:26-27, ESV) Jesus is called the "Great Physician". He literally does spiritual surgery! How amazing is His power. How great is His love! We are unable to love God or keep His commandments without His Spirit living inside of us.

Without a true born-again experience, we become religious converts. The difference is about 18 inches of space between our head and our hearts. We keep the rules of God's commandments but internally we have never been changed. This would be considered as the difference between head knowledge and heart transformation. This again goes back to the Garden of Eden. This is the difference between the Tree of Life and the Tree of the Knowledge of Good and Evil. When Jesus comes into our lives and our hearts, there is a true transformation. We stop doing things that we used to do that are displeasing to God. It is not out of force, but because we love Him and because it comes of the new spiritual nature that His Holy Spirit has brought into our lives:

"Whosoever is born of God doth not commit sin;
for his seed remaineth in him: and he cannot sin,

because he is born of God. In this the children of God are manifest, and the children of the devil: whosoever doeth not righteousness is not of God, neither he that loveth not his brother. For this is the message that ye heard from the beginning, that we should love one another." (1 John 3:9-11, KJV)

When we have that "born again" experience, it is now the Lord that does the transforming from the inside out. The difference is that Satan works from the outside in. It is the Lord who changes us from glory to glory. It is the process of sanctification. In other words, I am better today than I was yesterday. We desire to please God because He gives us a new heart that desires to keep His commandments and obey Him. It is a literal super-natural surgery!

We no longer live by our senses—that is, our flesh—but by the Spirit of the Living God. When we love someone, it is not a duty or grievous to do what pleases them. This should also be the attitude of our hearts towards our relationship with Jesus. His are not grievous commandments. Being good is not enough for God to allow us into heaven. Sadly, there are many "good" people in hell.

"We are all infected and impure with sin. When we display our righteous deeds, they are nothing but filthy rags. Like autumn leaves, we wither and fall, and our sins sweep us away like the wind." (Isaiah 64:6, NLT)

"For this is the love of God, that we keep His commandments; and His commandments are not burdensome." (1 John 5:3, NKJV)

<u>Life Lessons Study</u>

1. *<u>Have you ever seen food that looked good but tasted horrible? Describe it:</u>*

2. *<u>Have you ever met a person who appeared holy but was not? Explain:</u>*

3. *<u>What sins do you struggle with that you have a hard time overcoming?</u>*

4. *<u>What kinds of things feel good but are inconsistent with the scriptures?</u>*

5. *<u>What would the payoff be if you let go of a particular sin?</u>*

6. *<u>What are the steps you can take to get help in this area of your life?</u>*

7. *<u>Who caused Eve to sin in the Garden?</u>*

8. *<u>Why did Adam and Eve sin against God?</u>*

9. *<u>What is the answer for the battles of our flesh?</u>*

10. *<u>Why do we have a sinful nature?</u>*

Chapter 11

In Language...

"But the LORD came down to see the city and the tower the people were building. The LORD said, "If as one people speaking the same language they have begun to do this, then nothing they plan to do will be impossible for them. Come, let us go down and confuse their language so they will not understand each other." (Genesis 11:5, NIV)

Your inner consciousness becomes one with the force of this universe. The divine nature of God exists in all of us. When we look deep within ourselves, we connect with God's kingdom as His children. We are all God's children. I am one with him and he is one with me. God exists in each of us and is in everything. Love is the ultimate force. We have the power within us to reach our destiny. Your higher self-consciousness can attain your destiny. Your lower self knows it own illusions that pass away. We regard Him as the author of a divine plan, the natural law through which the universe, which He created, is governed and based on love, not fear.

That was the type of language I spoke before I became a Christian. The words above sound godly, but they are not. Many of these words, and this type of communication, are used by the New Agers and other counterfeit Christian religions. They claim to be Christian but they are not. I was involved for more than half of my life in the New Age systems of belief. I thought I knew God, but it was all an idol that I had made up in my own mind. The words used above sound spiritual but they can lead us into deep deception. Language as a communication system is thought to be fundamentally different from, and of much higher complexity than, those of other species. It is based on a complex system of rules relating symbols to their meanings resulting in an indefinite number of possible innovative utterances from a finite number of elements.

Most religions outside of the Christian faith used the scriptures in the Bible mixed along with their own teachings. For instance, one approach is to give respect to the Bible but teach that it cannot be fully trusted. They teach for example that books must have been lost or that texts were altered. They then offer other authoritative books (additional revelations) as Scriptures. The Mormon and many New Age groups are examples. They use the language of the scriptures but their teachings do not line up with sound Biblical doctrine. In many "so-called" Christian circles, ministers of the Gospel are slightly twisting the truth to do Satan's bidding. Let's take a look at this for an example:

1. Choose a sacred word as the symbol of your intention to consent to God's presence and action within. Examples: God, Jesus, Abba, Father, Mother, Mary, Amen. (Other

possibilities: Love, Peace, Mercy, Listen, Let Go, Silence, Stillness, Faith, Trust, Yes.)

2. Sitting comfortably and with eyes closed, settle briefly and silently introduce the sacred word as the symbol of your consent to God's presence and action within.

3. When engaged with your thoughts, return ever-so gently to the sacred word.

4. At the end of the prayer period, remain in silence with eyes closed for a couple of minutes. (Thoughts include body sensations, feelings, images, and reflections)

Ideally, the prayer will reach a point where the person no longer engaged in their thoughts as they arrive in their stream of consciousness. Are we saying that ministries are purposefully leading people into altered states of consciousness in order to introduce people to demonic spirits? No, we are not implying that they are purposefully attempting to do this. I am simply making the point that occultists and non-Christian mystics, who are in touch with demon spirits, use the same exact technique as Christian Contemplatives and "centering prayer" advocates. Perhaps, instead, we should say, proponents of the Contemplative prayer methodology are doing exactly what occultists and mystics have been doing for centuries, only now it is Christianized. It is important to note that self-induction into an altered state of consciousness is extremely dangerous. Christian mystics have done this through the centuries and they are doing it today. Hi-jacking Eastern spirituality (Buddhist, Hindu, etc.) in the name of Christianity, as a means to "connect with the Divine" and "have an experience", is evil. Yes, people are having "experiences" when they do these things but, to be sure, they are not "connecting" with the God of the Bible. Let the reader forever remember that the world of the occult is centered around spirituality based on experience, not on Biblical truth. Contrary to the schemes of the Prince of Darkness, the kingdom of our Lord God and Savior Jesus Christ is based on worshipping God "in spirit and in truth". Jesus said to the woman at the well: *"God is a Spirit: and they that worship him must worship him in spirit and in truth"* (John 4:24, KJV)

Have you heard of the "Word of Faith" movement? There is a danger within this movement with half truths. Basically they teach that if you "speak" it, it will happen. Name it and claim it they say. We as Christians must never tell God or command what He must do. He is God and we are His humble servants. We can pray and have faith to believe God and His Word, but we should never "demand" money, cars, wealth, a mate, manifestations, health and so on. Jesus himself said:

> *"Lay up not for yourselves treasures upon earth, where moth and rust doth corrupt, and where thieves break through and steal: But lay up for yourselves treasures in heaven, where neither moth nor rust doth corrupt, and where thieves do not break through and steal: for where your treasure is, there will your heart be also." (Matthew 6:19-21, KJV)*

God is the only one who creates. He "spoke" the worlds into existence. We are not the "creators". Clear scripture passages are altered to fit the Word-Faith system to establish the believer as one who possesses the divine nature so that he can realize his "legal authority." With this realization comes the knowledge, power, and ability of God. They believe you can "walk as Jesus walked, without any consciousness of inferiority to God or Satan. They also believe the Word of God conceived in the heart, formed by the tongue, and spoken out of the mouth is creative power. ...The spoken Word will work for you as you continually confess it", they say. Fear and guilt usually work in a downward spiral. One feels guilty because of a supposed lack of faith, then afraid because the confession is not "working." Then there is more guilt, then more fear, and so on, down into further despair. This cycle can be extremely debilitating both spiritually and physically. All of these spiritual and psychological difficulties can be directly attributed to elevating man to the false position of being a god and saying that he has powers far greater than he really does.

> *"For such men are false apostles, deceitful workmen, disguising themselves as apostles of Christ." (2 Corinthians 11:13, NASB)*

This is one of the many examples of how dangerous twisting the Word of God can be. Let take a look now at how our language can be deceptive in many forms.

SAY WHAT YOU MEAN, MEAN WHAT YOU SAY

It is not only the fruit of people's deeds that mark them

as false, but also the fruit of their words. The words of love, hatred, bitterness, perversion, and grace flow from our tongues and they are a pretty good indicator of what is in our heart.

> *"It is not what enters into the mouth that defiles the man, but what proceeds out of the mouth, this defiles the man." (Matthew 15:11, NASB)*

The stereo-type of a used car salesman is that he will tell you whatever you want to hear so that you will buy the car. Years ago in my life, a young man came in with smooth word of flattery and deception. He looked very sweet and handsome and the smooth words of his mouth were almost spell-binding. He ended up causing much pain and abuse that would have never happened if I knew better how to discern the true from the false. The con-artist is a revisionist and in using deceit must hide the evidence to make the lie stick.

> *"He who hates disguises it with his lips, But he lays up deceit in his heart. When he speaks graciously, do not believe him, for there are seven abominations in his heart." (Proverbs 26: 24-25, NASB)*

To be a good con-artist, you must cultivate certain mental-attitude sins, such as implacability, vindictiveness, and cruelty, as well as verbal sins such as flattery and lying (Judges 16:4-21). Samson had to deal with this with Delilah. She flattered him and then she could not believe that he would not tell her the truth. Deceiving Samson into believing she loved him, Delilah persuaded him to tell her the secret of his strength which was his long hair, the symbol of his Nazarite vow. While Samson slept at her home in the Valley of Sorek, the Philistines entered and cut his hair. With his strength gone, Samson was easily captured and imprisoned, and his eyes put out. She deceived Samson by feigning to be upset with him for not telling the truth!

All of us, at sometime, will fail because inevitably the very thing that makes us strong—honor and integrity—also make us vulnerable and sometimes even weak. We begin to assume that everyone who is nice, everyone who is well-mannered, and everyone who knows the vocabulary of believers in Jesus Christ is somehow just as honorable, just as honest, filled with the same level of integrity that we have—and that's when things really begin to fall apart!

How many times have we spoken to a person with contempt and bitterness in our hearts? If we are not quick to repent to the person we have wounded or betrayed it will harden out hearts. We have a habit of reasoning away our sins and excusing them. As a woman in ministry, I have encountered many men in Christian circles who have a habit of yelling, raging, sexually exploiting, belittling my knowledge, making continual sexual remarks, threatening, disrespecting my position, and cunningly wanting to be close to me because of the position the God has given me in public ministry. These behaviors are no different than those of the world. Behind closed doors, Christian ministry has become defiled to the core. I listen to what a person says with their mouth to know what is in their hearts. Purity has become almost non-existent whether in word or in deed. It is deceptive to the core. If there is a point where a person is not convicted of what comes out of their mouth, they are in danger spiritually. It is a true saying, "a man is good as his word". We can speak the Christian lingo, and be far from God's heart.

"but no human being can tame the tongue. It is a restless evil, full of deadly poison. With the tongue we praise our Lord and Father, and with it we curse human beings, who have been made in God's likeness." (James 3:8-9, NIV)

What about speaking half-truths? A half truth is a lie. Deception occurs in relationships, ministries, and spiritually when we operate in or believe in a half truth. We must all stand before the judgment seat of Christ and give an account for every idle word we speak (Matthew 12:36).This should be a very sobering thought for each one of us.

Most Christians are not familiar with Greek and Hebrew nor the way to study the scriptures with objective study helps. Many people do not even read a whole book in the Bible through for its intended context. Therefore, when a false teacher comes with a plausible argument and presents what appears to be a scholarly approach, the novice is impressed by that person's intelligence and knowledge through their words. It is NOT wise to believe a person this way. Everything must be lined up with sound Biblical doctrine...the Word of God.

WORDS OF LIFE

"The Spirit gives life; the flesh counts for nothing. The words I have spoken to you are spirit and they are life." (John 6:63, NIV)

God's Word is fit to produce or give life to the soul dead in sins. Jesus speaks life to us. He said that He is the Way, the Truth and the Life. When we are desperate to know the truth and we find it, it will set us free (John 8:32). Truth is not based on what we or others say but only what the Word of God says. To be doctrinally sound, we must take the Word "literally" to keep us from deception. Many people are swayed by the smooth talk of deceivers and are swept away to spiritual deception because they did not love the truth. People have exchanged the truth of God for a lie (Romans 1:25). What some people believe is truly amazing.

People are able to believe weird lies because they do not love the truth:

"The coming of the lawless one is according to the working of Satan, with all power, signs, and lying wonders, and with all unrighteous deception among those who perish, because they did not receive the love of the truth, that they might be saved. And for this reason God will send them strong delusion, that they should believe the lie, that they all may be condemned

who did not believe the truth but had pleasure in unrighteousness." (2 Thessalonians 2:9-12, NKJV)

Some people know the truth, but do not obey it:

"But in accordance with your hardness and your impenitent heart you are treasuring up for yourself wrath in the day of wrath and revelation of the righteous judgment of God, who 'will render to each one according to his deeds': eternal life to those who by patient continuance in doing good seek for glory, honor, and immortality; but to those who are self-seeking and do not obey the truth, but obey unrighteousness—indignation and wrath." (Romans 2:5-8, NKJV)

Some even seek out teachers who will tell them pleasing lies!

"For the time will come when they will not endure sound doctrine, but according to their own desires, because they have itching ears, they will heap up for themselves teachers; and they will turn their ears away from the truth, and be turned aside to fables." (2 Timothy 4:3-4, NKJV)

"For there are many insubordinate, both idle talkers and deceivers, especially those of the circumcision, whose mouths must be stopped, who

subvert whole households, teaching things which they ought not, for the sake of dishonest gain. ... Therefore rebuke them sharply, that they may be sound in the faith, not giving heed to Jewish fables and commandments of men who turn from the truth" (Titus 1:10-14, NKJV)

Some people are always learning, but because of a wrong attitude, they never learn the truth:

"For of this sort are those who creep into households and make captives of gullible women loaded down with sins, led away by various lusts, always learning and never able to come to the knowledge of the truth. Now as James and Jambres resisted Moses, so do these also resist the truth: men of corrupt minds, disapproved concerning the faith" (2 Timothy 3:6-8, NKJV)

We know the truth through Jesus Christ:

"And the Word became flesh and dwelt among us, and we beheld His glory, the glory as of the only begotten of the Father, full of grace and truth" (John 1:14, NKJV).

"For the law was given through Moses, but grace and truth came through Jesus Christ" (John 1:17, NKJV).

"Jesus said to him, I am the way, the truth, and the life. No one comes to the Father except through Me" (John 14:6, NKJV).

Jesus came to tell us the truth. *"Pilate therefore said to Him, Are You a king then? Jesus answered, 'You say rightly that I am a king. For this cause I was born, and for this cause I have come into the world, that I should bear witness to the truth. Everyone who is of the truth hears My voice"* (John 18:37, NKJV).

For spiritual purification we must obey the truth:

"Since you have purified your souls in obeying the truth through the Spirit in sincere love of the brethren, love one another fervently with a pure heart, having been born again, not of corruptible seed but incorruptible, through the word of God which lives and abides forever" (1 Peter 1:22-23, NKJV).

Christians must believe and know the truth (1 Timothy 4:3):

Jesus told His apostles: *"I still have many things to say to you, but you cannot bear them now. However, when He, the Spirit of truth, has come, He will guide you into all truth; for He will not speak on His own authority, but whatever He hears He will speak; and He will tell you things to come"* (John 16:12,13, NKJV).

The truth is revealed to us through the Scriptures. Jesus prayed: *"Sanctify them by Your truth. Your word is truth"* (John 17:17, NKJV). If we love the truth, we will search the Scriptures diligently to learn the truth. We will be like the Bereans: *"These were more fair minded than those in Thessalonica, in that they received the word with all readiness, and searched the Scriptures daily to find out whether these things were so"* (Acts 17:11, NKJV).

We must handle the Scriptures correctly:

Always remember to study the Scriptures… *"Be diligent to present yourself approved to God, a worker who does not need to be ashamed, rightly dividing the word of truth."* (2 Timothy 2:15, NKJV)

As you read the scriptures, you can now understand why knowing and speaking the truth is a very serious matter in God's sight. Your language must be the true Word of God. It is pure, infallible and eternal.

> *"Death and life are in the power of the tongue:*
> *and they that love it shall eat the fruit thereof."*
> *(Proverbs 18:21, KJV)*

Life Lessons Study

1. *What motivates a person to twist the solid teaching of the scriptures?*

2. *How can we identify if a person is speaking false doctrine?*

3. *Have you ever been seduced by someone's words?*

4. *How can language be used to manipulate truth?*

5. *How can Satan use the scriptures to deceive you?*

6. *Name some religions that use the Bible but are false religions:*

7. *Write 5 words that best describe your safeguard from spiritual deception?*

8. *Give an example when you have used words to harm or heal another person:*

9. *Who's words can you count on that will never deceive you? Why?*

10. *List some characteristics of someone who deceives with biblical language?*

Chapter 12

In Good Deeds…

—⚜—

s a young woman, my family would take me to the Sikh Temple (Gurdwara) from time to time. Gurdwara means the "guru's door". The men and women would take off their shoes and cover their heads while entering into the service. As you walked in and sat down, you had to approach the **Guru Granth** *(the Sikh scripture is considered to be the living guru of the Sikhs). In every Gurdwara, the Sikh place of worship, the Guru Granth is kept on a platform in a prominent place. Sikhs worshiping at the Gurdwara bow before Guru Granth before sitting down. When I looked around, I always thought there was something missing. I did not know what it was at that time. Everyone appeared religious in their appearance and I also felt like a better person for being at a religious service.*

In every man and woman born, there is a nature of the beast which seeks to draw attention to itself. In a world full of different religions and many cultures, a person has a need and a craving to feel good about themselves. Most people basically consider themselves a "good person." In fact, most people believe that they will go to heaven if, in fact, they even believe there is such a place. This belief is centered around the Tree of Knowledge which is found in the Garden of Eden. Self-centeredness is the problem that afflicts most of us. We will have a dead religion with righteousness which is based on the obeying the written commandments instead of a living relationship with our God. The fallen nature in man desires to "feel good" about itself, and thus, every good deed propagates his belief system. There are many "good causes" in our world today (e.g., feeding the poor, pro life organizations, feeding and clothing the homeless, caring for the elderly, missions work, etc.). Even the most moral and upstanding citizens in Israel crucified Jesus. Abortion is a horror but it is a symptom of a much deeper problem. Homosexuality is a flagrant perversion, but it is still a symptom. Hitler had many "good" qualities but he was responsible for the killing of 6 million Jews.

The word "legalism" does not occur in the Bible. It is a term Christians use to describe a doctrinal position emphasizing a system of rules and regulations for achieving both salvation and spiritual growth. Legalists believe in and demand a strict literal adherence to rules and regulations. Doctrinally, it is a position essentially opposed to grace. Those who hold a legalistic position often fail to see the real purpose for law, especially the purpose of the Old Testament law of Moses, which is to be our "schoolmaster" or "tutor" to bring us to Christ (Galatians 3:24).

Most religions, including Christians, highly esteem those in our society who have high success, moral excellence and the most conservative. While I was growing up, I was always compared to the other girls who were prettier, smarter and married with children. India's society is rooted in pride. If you have a doctoral degree and are well respected in the community, then you are highly favored. This type of influence caused me to feel as though I was never "good" enough". Not good enough in God's eyes and definitely not in man's eyes. I kept "trying" to do better so that I would be accepted by family and friends but I kept falling short. When a person tries to do good to be accepted by man, it is a never ending quest.

When I was a child, my father abandoned our family. My mother was in a new country without friends or an education to take care of me and my 2 brothers. I remember during my rebellious teenage years, she called my father and asked him to help me. I will never forget the words he said as I was listening quietly on the phone. He said, "I want nothing to do with her." He was my father. I was 16 years old when this happened. After that phone call, I went into a downward spiral desperately longing for acceptance by my family and the world. I never saw him again, nor have I heard his voice since that day. I was told that he passed away many years ago.

Hopeless Approval

With suicide rates and mental illness at an all time high, it is crucial that each person truly takes a look at the root of the problem. Before I became a Christian, I tried to commit suicide three times. My life was empty and I had no hope for a future. I felt like I was never good enough, I could not stop the torment and I continually failed at everything I did. Because of these feelings, I began making a series of wrong decisions. When we try to gain approval from man, we become consumed with performance or good works. Our life becomes a stage of living for others to prove we are good. *"There is no one who does good, not even one"* (Psalms 14:3, NIV). We become our own worst enemy.

There is a medication now for every spiritual, emotional and physical symptom. Even in churches, there is a group for almost every dysfunction and addiction. Groups can help with sharing and accountability, but only Jesus can set us free. We as Christians do not believe in behavior modification. It is short lived. My theory is: There is a devil on the loose and sin is the root problem for approval. Man's nature must change. Even the greatest compassion and good works of man is to atone for his evil and for him to justify that he does not need Christ. The goodness of man can be the most rebellious form of evil rooted in pride and deception.

> *"All of us have become like one who is unclean, and all our righteous acts are like filthy rags; we all shrivel up like a leaf, and like the wind our sins sweep us away." (Isaiah 64:6, NIV)*

A man is tempted to think that he's made it if he can just outdo some other man in terms of achievement, wealth, or other kind of competition. Much of this attitude is so ingrained in us that we don't even have to consciously decide to compete and compare. We do it unceasingly and without even noticing it. We subconsciously chase after the wind, and we have become enslaved to a temptation of the devil. We are trying to find our worth and identity not based in how God values us, but in what others think of us. This is why we glorify and even deify sports stars, Hollywood icons, pop artists, and media elites.

We constantly live under the illusion of if only I did this, had this, made this, knew so-and-so, became like so-and-so, and got this, then I would get so-and-so's approval and then I would be happy. Such is the ridiculous notion of trying to catch the wind. It can never be done, for it is impossible. In fact, it was ordained and designed to fail. Such is supposed to draw us to the only true source of satisfaction, wholeness, healing, and fulfillment—which is Jesus Christ. It is all by God's design. Hopefully, we have come to the point where we get sick and tired of trying to people-please, worrying about peer pressure, and trying to outdo our neighbor.

Solomon, the wisest man who ever live, said, remarking of life, in general, said, *"I have seen that every labor and every skill which is done is the result of rivalry between a man and his neighbor.* This too is vanity and striving after wind" (Ecclesiastes 4:4, NASB). As is the futility of chasing the mythical pot of gold at the end of the rainbow, trying to find our worth based upon human rank, performance, or others' acceptance is never going to satisfy or fulfill the void that rejection and hurt has left in our hearts. It is a striving after the wind.

The Pharisees wanted the approval of men, so they acted in a way that would attract attention to themselves, in a way that would make them look righteous, as men might judge it. The Pharisees were into long prayers, they visibly fasted and made contributions, and took the places of prominence at banquets and the like. Their clothing, too, was ostentatious—they lengthened their phylacteries. The Pharisees were repulsed by the fact that Jesus associated with sinners, and even ate with them. They were proud of the fact that they kept their distance. No defilement for them! They meticulously washed themselves ceremonially, and they observed Sabbath regulations. In all of this, Jesus said, they were hypocrites, because their hearts were wicked, because they were not really righteous at all.

> *"Outwardly you look like righteous people, but inwardly your hearts are filled with hypocrisy and lawlessness." (Matthew 23:28, NLT)*

When God Approves

The approval of God is different from the approval of man. I realized this when I finally gave my life to Jesus Christ. The Lord Jesus has been speaking to the crowds, among whom were the Pharisees. They are not at all pleased with what they have seen and heard from Jesus. They grumbled against Jesus for receiving sinners and even eating with them (Luke 15:2). In response to this, Jesus told three parables, all of which dealt with the finding of something lost. While the Pharisees could identify with the rejoicing of one who found something material (a lost sheep or a coin), they could not rejoice in the return of a repentant sinner, even though all of heaven did so. This is because they hated grace. They did not believe they needed grace, and they did not appreciate it being manifested to anyone else, especially the undeserving (which are always the recipients of grace). If Jesus was out of step with the Pharisees, they were out of step with God and with heaven.

"For they loved the glory that comes from man more than the glory that comes from God." John 12:43, ESV)

We cannot attain heaven by good works. Why chase the approval of man? Why look to earthly things to fill a void that only Jesus can fill? Why constantly compete to look better than someone else? Someone will always be better at something, or more beautiful, or more successful than we are. Rather, we ought to enjoy what God has given us to do and do it to the best of our ability to God's glory. Colossians 3:23 says, *"Whatever you do, do your work heartily, as for the Lord rather than for men."* (NASB) When we come to the point where we view everything as an act of worship to God, we will finally ignore the approval of man. When what God says is the only verdict that matters, man's opinions won't matter any longer. May God bring us each to the place where we are cognizant of doing all things for Him no matter what it may cost us. May He enable us to stop worrying about what others might think if we do what is right and just.

Besides the fact that man's approval doesn't satisfy, why else should we live for God's glory rather than for our own glory by chasing after the approval of man? Colossians 3:24 continues, *"knowing that from the Lord you will receive the reward of the inheritance. It is the Lord Christ whom you serve."* (NASB) The great equalizer is the justice of God; all men will have to stand before His throne. Our neighbor with the bigger house, yard, and boat is not going to judge us. Our supervisor who has the authority to promote, demote, or fire us is not going to judge us. Our spouse or family member, whose approval we so dearly want, is not going to judge us. Yet the temptation to seek their approval over God's is so great. Only God will be the judge, and only He has the power and authority to give out rewards. It is He alone whom we are to serve.

We can't serve both God and man or money or anything else that this world seeks. At the end of the day — at the end of life — it makes no sense to live in enslavement to people-pleasing. Since God is the only one whose opinion ultimately matters, and who has the power to give out rewards that last forever, we ought only to concern ourselves with pleasing Him. We can handle rejection by men for the sake of God if we know that God will honor us for doing so in eternity. We must appreciate the glory of eternal honor over temporary earthly honor.

Our own righteousness, based on the Law, brings us into direct conflict with the "Truth". In fact, we become persecutors of the true worshippers when we live by the Law. Cain was jealous of Abel because his brother's works were accepted by God while his were not. The righteousness of God is completely based on the atonement of Jesus on the cross and His sacrifice. All of those who come to the cross are stripped of self-righteousness and pride. In other words, there is NOTHING we can do or nothing we can give to receive Jesus to have God's approval. When we acknowledge that there is nothing good in us that we have to offer to God, then and only then, have we come to the real truth. The cross is the greatest threat to man's self centeredness.

To avoid falling into the trap of legalism, we can start by holding fast to the words of the Apostle John, *"For the law was given through Moses; grace and truth came through Jesus Christ"* (John 1:17, NASB) and remembering to be gracious, especially to our brothers and sisters in Christ. *"Who are you to judge someone else's servant? To his own master he stands or falls. And he will stand, for the Lord is able to make him stand"* (Romans 14:4, NIV). *"You, then, why do you judge your brother? Or why do you look down on your brother? For we will all stand before God's judgment seat"* (Romans 14:10, NIV).

A word of caution is necessary here. While we need to be gracious to one another and tolerant of disagreement over disputable matters, we cannot accept heresy. We are exhorted to contend for the faith that was once for all entrusted to the saints (Jude 3). If we remember these guidelines and apply them in love and mercy, we will be safe from both legalism and heresy.

> *"Dear friends, do not believe every spirit, but test the spirits to see whether they are from God, because many false prophets have gone out into the world"* (1 John 4:1, *NIV).*

> *"More than that, I count all things to be loss in view of the surpassing value of knowing Christ Jesus my Lord, for whom I have suffered the loss of all things, and count them but rubbish so that I may gain Christ, and may be found in Him, not having a righteousness of my own derived from the Law, but that which is through faith in*

Christ, the righteousness which comes from God on the basis of faith." (Philippians 3:8-9, NASB)

Life Study Lessons

1. *What roles do good deeds play in the life of a Christian?*

2. *What was the last good deed someone did for you and how did it make you feel?*

3. *Why will good people go to hell?*

4. *Do you believe God loves you? Why?*

5. *What's more important—the deed or the motive behind the deed? Discuss:*

6. *How does Satan lie to you about doing good deeds to get God's approval?*

7. *Does God approve of you and why?*

8. *Whose approval have you fought for but have never obtained?*

9. *What is the difference between "grace" and "works"?*

10. *Give an example "Grace" in the Bible:*

Closing Remarks...

*"Therefore go and make disciples of all nations,
baptizing them in the name of the Father and of the
Son and of the Holy Spirit." (Matthew 28:19, NIV)*

I have enjoyed sharing not only the experiences in my
life but also the truths that the Holy Spirit has revealed
to me. God can use the weak of this world to confound the
wise...someone like me.

*"But God chose the foolish things of the world
to shame the wise; God chose the weak things of
the world to shame the strong. He chose the lowly
things of this world and the despised things—
and the things that are not—to nullify the things
that are, so that no one may boast before him."
(1 Corinthians 1:27-29, NIV)*

There is a great deception that is coming upon the earth
and it is already at work. It is called the spirit of anti-Christ.
My greatest desire is not to condemn those reading this book
but only to share the truth of God's Word. If we love people,

we will tell them the "Truth". It will not be our truth but God's truth. We must have the love of God for those that are lost. Our souls must cry out for those that are lost. If this element is missing, it is because there is someone missing in our hearts. The King of Kings and the Lord of Lords. It is important for each one of us not only to test everything that I have written against the Word of God, but also to study the scriptures.

Jesus warned us of so many things that will take place as the end of time draws near. We must be sober and alert. If your heart has been touched by this book and you have the conviction of the Holy Spirit that something is not right within you, then please listen to the voice of Jesus. It is never too late until our last breath. There is no sin so deep that Jesus is not deeper still. He will give you ever-lasting life. We will all live forever. But where we spend eternity is based on whether or not we receive the sacrifice of Jesus on the cross for our sins or reject His free gift of salvation.

He will remove the blinders from your eyes and heart. He is your peace. He is your salvation. His love for you is everlasting no matter what you have done. No matter how evil or simple...sin is sin. The only difference between sins is that some sins have greater consequences than others in this life—yet both end in judgment and eternal separation from God. I am asking that you choose not to die in your sins. Jesus is the sacrifice for our sins. He died on the cross and paid the penalty for your sins. If you receive Him and His sacrifice, you can go directly to the Father in Jesus name and through His shed blood. Pray with me:

Heavenly Father,

Please forgive me. I have sinned against you. I have broken your laws and commandments. I ask for your mercy. Wash me in the blood of Jesus of all of my sins. Forgive me of all of my unrighteousness. I repent of my sins and turn away from them and I turn to you. Jesus, come into my heart and be the Lord and Savior of my life. I receive you right now. I give you my life. I surrender my life to you. Fill me with your Holy Spirit. I renounce the kingdom of Satan and every parcel ground I have given him in my life. My life belongs to you Jesus. I am yours now. Thank you for your mercy and grace toward me. Thank you that my name is now written in the Lamb's Book of Life. In Jesus' Name I pray...Amen.

*"For God so loved the world, that He gave His only begotten Son, that **whoever** believes in Him will not perish, but have eternal life" (John 3:16, NASB)*

It is important to get involved in a Bible believing church and to have fellowship with others Christians. It is important now to study the Word of God and also have a prayer life. We would love to hear how this book impacted your life. If you have received Jesus as your Lord and Savior, please contact us and share your testimony. God Bless you now and forever more!

Yasmeen Suri can be reached at www.yasmeensuri.com. Other materials are also available on the website. If you have any questions regarding these, or others topics, please feel free to contact us directly. For all other inquiries, please visit the website.

You are not a mistake. God created you. Remember that God has a plan and purpose for your life!

Acknowledgements

I would like to acknowledge and express gratitude to the following people that have had an impact on my life.

My wonderful Church family at Brightmoor Christian Church and many of the people that keep me covered in prayer and friendship.

Thank you, Pastor Jamie and Kim Kjos for preaching and teaching the Word of God without compromise and for your impact on my life.

All of the people who help support Praise from the Nations Int'l Ministries from around the world, not only in giving of their time, but also of their resources.

My closest friend and mentor Patricia Curley who has been my biggest support and who has prayed with me and interceded for me for many years.

The countless television and radio programs that the Lord has used to share my story and testimony across the globe.

Thank you Raphael Damian Martinez and Randy Vaughan for the countless hours you have put into this book and for your inspiration and theological knowledge of God's Word.

My many pastors and many personal friends who have

encouraged me to press unto the high call of God.

A special thanks to Pastor Loran Livingston from Central Church of God. Thank you for having such a powerful impact on my life when I was first saved. I am forever grateful for you.

Most of all, I am eternally grateful to my Lord and Savior Jesus Christ who has delivered me from the hand of the enemy by shedding His own blood for me. Thank you Lord, for giving me the patience and endurance to write this book. May it accomplish Your will in the lives of men and women in Jesus name…amen.

Notes...

Bible Scripture Translations: ESV - KJV - NASB - NIV - NKJV - NLT - RSV

Christian Apologetics and Research Ministry: "What is the New Age Movement?"

Notes taken from taped messages by Pastor R. B. Thieme, Berachah Church - Houston, Texas.

TurnbacktoGod.com Lucifer – Article: "Angel of Music"

Elliot Miller: How "New Age" is new age music Article: DN389

FBC Springfield.net – "Worship"

End Times Information: File:Wordpress.com

The Enslavement of Seeking Man's Approval - ReveleantBibleteaching.com

Roy Davidson – "Old Path Archives"

Contemplative Method Outreach, Washington – "Prayer Method"

Gotquestions.org- Christians – "Legalism"

Lynette Woods – Article: "Judging and Discerning"

Cult Awareness and Information Library

Ronnie Mutina – Article: "Chosen by God"

Apologeticsindex.org

J. Hampton Keathley, III - From the Series: "Marks of Maturity: Biblical Characteristics of a Christian Leader"

Diane S. Dew – Article: "Signs and Wonders"

Barry L. Brumfield –Article: "The strong delusion of God"

Betty Miller – Article: "What does the Bible say about Lying Signs and Wonders?"

Christianbiblereference.org

Bob and Gretchen Passantino – Article: "Truth and Consequences: Exposing Sin in the Church"

Cooper P. Abrams 111 – Article: "Does God speak to men and Dreams and Visions today?"

Tom Stewart - Article: "How to identify a False Prophet"

Marsha West - Article "Televangelists snicker all the way to the bank"

Betterthansacrifice.org – Article: "False Doctrine Destroys Christian Unity"

Dan Corner - "Christian Unity" – Evangelical Outreach Box 265 Washington, PA 15301

Ed Merritt - Mission Venture Ministries – Wordpress

Damon Whitsell – Article: "Fleecing the Flock" – Wordpress

Propheticministries.org

Eric Johnson – Article: 8 Characteristics of a Counterfeit Christian Church

Julie Ferwerda – Article: "Do Prophets Still Exist Today?"

Steve Cable - "Seeing through Media Bias" Probe Ministries 2001 W. Plano Parkway, Suite 2000 Plano TX 75075

Vigilantcitizen.com – Article: "Mind Control Theories and Techniques used by Mass Media"

ukapologetics.net: Copyright Robin A. Brace 2003 "Are there

really prophets today in our church?"

United Church of God – Article: "The Rise of a Counterfeit Christianity"

Theologic.com: Article: *Reprinted from the OCA's The Resource Handbook, 1982, No. 2.* © 1996 by Orthodox Family Life and the original author(s)

CPSIA information can be obtained
at www.ICGtesting.com
Printed in the USA
LVHW090742210619
621814LV00026B/171/P

9 781625 095701